Cars Detroit Never Built

Cars Detroit Never Built

FIFTY YEARS OF AMERICAN EXPERIMENTAL CARS

Edward Janicki

A Sterling/Main Street Book
Sterling Publishing Co., Inc.   New York

To my wife, Sylvia,
and children, Michael, Donna and Gregory

10 9 8 7 6 5 4 3 2

A Sterling/Main Street Book

Copyright © 1990 by Edward Janicki
Published by Sterling Publishing Company, Inc.,
387 Park Avenue South, New York, N.Y. 10016.
Distributed in Canada by Sterling Publishing,
c/o Canadian Manda Group, P.O. Box 920, Station U,
Toronto, Ontario, Canada M8Z 5P9.
Distributed in Great Britain and Europe by Cassell PLC,
Villiers House, 41/47 Strand, London WC2N 5JE, England.
Distributed in Australia by Capricorn Ltd.,
P.O. Box 665, Lane Cove, NSW 2066.

Designed by Ronald R. Misiur

Sterling ISBN 0-8069-7424-9

Library of Congress Cataloging-in-Publication Data

Janicki, Edward.
   Cars Detroit never built: Fifty years of American experimental cars / Edward Janicki
      p.   cm.
   ISBN 0-8069-7424-9
   1. Experimental automobiles–United States–History. I. Title.
TL23.J36 1990
629.222–dc20
                                          90-37027
                                          CIP

Contents

Introduction

They're all gone now—most of them dismantled, destroyed, forgotten. A few of them are collecting dust in the labs. Some are in museums. They were the experimental cars of the past, cars which we all got a glimpse of at auto shows, but never got to drive. Each was exciting, different from the next. They were one-of-a-kind vehicles which were never put into production. They came on the scene briefly, then fell into oblivion.

Their purpose: To test the public's acceptance of new ideas. There were more than 100 of these "idea" cars built since 1938.

That was the year that General Motors Corp. built the first "dream" or experimental car, under the direction of the late Harley J. Earl, GM's genius vice president of styling. Called the "Y-Job," it began a parade of futuristic cars which have excited millions of people in America and abroad. The dream car became a world-famous symbol of the motoring public's evergrowing fascination with the life it could expect in the future. The dream car has been far more than a gleaming automobile on a pedestal—it has brought tremendous benefits to every motorist. It stimulated the stylist to creative thinking because it allowed him to build in three dimensions the futuristic ideas he conceived which were too advanced to be applied to the design of next year's model. This caught and brought to life for the motorist many design ideas which might otherwise have been lost.

Once built and exhibited, the dream car made it possible to gauge public reaction to its new features through customer research. This evidence of acceptability encouraged a manufacturer to spend the money to put an idea into production far sooner than he might if he had doubts about its acceptance.

The 1938 Y-Job had a host of "firsts," including the first electrically operated convertible top, first power windows, the first extension of fenders into the front doors, and the first concealed running board. After being shown across the country and tested extensively, it was "retired" to a GM warehouse.

World War II stopped Detroit auto makers from dreaming and forced them to concentrate on military production. It wasn't until thirteen years later—in 1951—that the second GM experimental car made its appearance—the famous LeSabre, which could use either premium gas or methyl alcohol and had built-in hydraulic tire jacks.

There was also a Buick XP-300 concept car introduced that year which had an all-aluminum body and boasted many features similar to the LeSabre's. Since then, General Motors alone has created at least one model each year, thirteen alone in 1954. Ford and Chrysler also displayed their imaginations with scores of futuristic experimental cars.

While the number of "dream cars" auto companies have presented for public viewing has declined since that activity reached its peak in the mid- and late Fifties, it is by no means an indication that work on experimental cars has been forgotten. With the advent of the two energy crises and recessions of the 70's and early 80's, show car expressions did enter a fallow era where not much of consequence was accomplished. But now new creative thinking is once again emerging from Detroit's design studios.

All the Big Three auto companies are still designing futuristic cars, some resembling lunar space ships. In the recent past there have been cars with only two wheels, and some with six. Next possible step: a solar-powered car. Auto companies around the world are now working on one.

Early in 1988 General Motors Corp. let fly with a new barrage of show cars, the Cadillac Voyage, Buick Lucerne, Chevrolet Venture, Oldsmoble Aerotech, Pontiac Pursuit, and even a "pickup truck" – the GMC Centaur. Chrysler Corp. came forth with an odd-looking vehicle called the "Slingshot," which represents an overt appeal to young life styles, and the Chrysler Portfolio, by Lamborghini, which explores the potential for an ultimate high speed functional luxury four-door sedan. Ford broke the new dawn of the decade with a continuum of "Probe" show cars that led to its most recent Probe V design.

Why weren't any of the "dream cars" of yesteryear put into production?

Says Charles Jordan, Vice President of the General Motors Corp. Design Staff: "A lot of concept cars that are developed in General Motors never see the light of day out in the public. They're for us and for our management and for the divisional management to bring us all along so that when we do a new production design, people are educated to it.

"We're all human—anything new looks strange, so you've got to put some things out there to get people used to them so that when the judgments are made on production cars you're not as conservative as you would be if you hadn't experienced this. So, that's why some of these concept cars never reach the light of day.

"On the other hand, some of these cars are purposely put out in public to get reactions to design—and to individual design features. And the reactions can be very clear and emphatic. You just go put the cars out in an auto show and stay tuned. Boy, they'll tell you in a hurry. In fact, that's a good way to sell a design. If we want to sell a design (inside), and we're having difficulty, we promote putting it in an auto show and if the thing is good and the demand is there somebody will say, "Hey, maybe we ought to be doing that."

"Now the other thing about concept cars is that they make an immediate statement that design is alive and well at General Motors. Believe me, that's happened. And it's happened with the current crop of concept cars.

These image cars, really, most of them are running cars. And they have a profound influence on where we're going. You'll see that over the next few years as our new models come out and you can compare them with the concept cars you're looking at today."

Notes Thomas C. Gale, Chrysler Corp. vice president of Product Design: "If some of those concept cars actually came into production, we probably wouldn't have reached far enough. A lot of small things that are going into production today came from those cars, like certain styling touches. In some case, for the years ahead, the industry is depending on future materials breakthroughs to really happen. Some of the things we have been doing have tremendous value for the future. With passive restraints and air bags coming into the picture, we're now even experimenting with different steering wheels.

"Another example is the modular approach to bumpers, which was shown on concept cars for many years, and we're starting to see a new philosophy in what we do with production cars in that respect. Instead of having a piece of bumper bolted onto the front end, now it is an integral part of the front end that goes all the way to the wheel openings with one very simple cut line. Also, there's been a trend in recent years to modular interiors, such as seats that curve into the side panels. That's something that is a direct lift from some of the things we were trying to do with show cars. Just look at what we've been able to do with composite, or plastic, parts as we go into the future. A lot of that came about because technology is really starting to catch up with what we were doing with show cars."

Further evidence that some of the innovations presented in experimental cars do eventually get into production is summarized by J. J. Telnack, Ford's vice president–design. He observes:

"Contrary to most people's beliefs, many features and design themes developed for concept vehicles do reach the public in production vehicles. Two or three that come to mind were Ford's Ghia Barchetta, which debuted at the 1983 Frankfurt, West Germany, Motor Show and the Ford Probe IV, which premiered at the 1983 Tokyo, Japan, Motor Show.

"The Ghia Barchetta tested public reaction to a very small, two-passenger sports car priced well below the current available competitors on the market. The response was overwhelming. Over 10,000 letters were received by Ford of Europe from the public praising the vehicle and requesting production plans! With public reaction of that strength, a full-bore production program code-named "SA-30" was initiated and the results can be seen . . . in the 1989 Lincoln-Mercury Capri. . . .

"The aerodynamic test vehicle, Probe IV, was developed to break the c/d record for four-door vehicles. The fully-driveable Probe IV's drag coefficient of .157 did break the old record and still holds it. Probably more importantly, the shape of Probe IV was very well received and led to a confirmation of theme for the 1986 Taurus and Sable.

"And of course, let's not forget the Ford of Europe-designed concept vehicle, Probe III, introduced at the 1981 Frankfurt Motor Show, was a sneak preview of the 1982 1/2 Sierra, or XR4 Ti as it is known as in this country. It was shown to the public just before final approval of the exterior design to insure that the aero-look would work in Europe. Public reaction at the show was positive and management then took the gamble and put the Sierra into production.

"I think the above illustrates that concept vehicles really do influence production cars and trucks. Speaking of trucks, the concept utility vehicle, Bronco DM-1, which debuted at the 1988 Detroit Auto Show, has been not only extremely popular here in the United States, but after its showing at the Geneva Motor show . . . , 1988 Bronco II's are now being imported and sold in Switzerland. Ford Motor Company will be building concept vehicles for a long time to come. Their value cannot be overstated."

Today the auto industry would rather forget some of the ideas it conceived in the 1950s and '60s, like sharp-pointed fins, bodies laden with chrome, and rocket-style front ends. It was a period of fantasy and had to come

to an end, like clothing fashions or any other mores that go in cycles.

Detroit designers, and everyone for that matter, agree that the 1950s and '60s were fun times in the auto industry. But the world of transportation has changed. Innovations are now more practical, sparked mainly by the fuel crisis and tougher U.S. government standards for safer cars–instead of cars that look like torpedoes with sword-like body designs enough to scare a dinosaur. Today, under government regulations, an automobile bumper must withstand so much shock and be designed according to government standards. Cars must give a certain mileage with one gallon of fuel, under CAFE standards (Corporate Automobile Fuel Economy). Exterior lights must be a certain height from the ground, and there are a multitude of interior design specifications, such as padding and location of gauges. Most of the autos of the 1950s and '60s would flunk those requirements.

Those gull-wing doors and plastic bubble tops of yesteryear are too expensive to produce and, besides, they have water leakage problems. Such flippant "Star Trek" concept cars are today a waste of time and money, and research is now more down to earth. The automobile business has changed drastically since the 1950s.

While many of the innovations that appeared on the experimental cars since 1938 have been radical, impractical, or too expensive, a few did find their way into production. Those that did were mainly electronic gadgets. Automatic cruise control, featured on a General Motors dream car in the 1940s, was one of them. Four-wheel steering is making its appearance, and control buttons for radio and other functions in the steering wheel can be found in present models. Some offer electronic maps in the dash. We even have remote keyless entry systems currently offered on some models. Some of the other more practical devices could still make the cut, if Detroit could reduce costs, and if the demand were there. "Talking cars," demonstrated by the industry in recent years, are making their way into actual production to a small extent. Car companies predict more such systems will be seen in cars during the coming years–a synthesized voice system and on-board computers that tell us verbally everything that needs attention on our cars. And if you think the cars of the past fifty years looked strange, they may become even stranger.

Here are some of the things that Detroit's top designers envision for the 21st Century:

Cars will get lighter, slicker, smaller, and more modular. Various tricks could be done with modules. Like using Lego plastic toy pieces, you'll be able to make almost any type of body you want, changing it from a sedan to a two-seater, pickup truck, or bus. The smaller cars will seat just one person and be powered by three cylinders. Grilles will become obsolete: they hinder aerodynamic efficiency. Vans will replace station wagons. Rust will become a dead issue, thanks to foreseeable advances in metal technology.

"Heads-up" displays will be commonplace, showing the driver the car's speed and condition on the windshield in line with his vision. (This system was actually offered on some 1989 cars to get public reaction).

Before the year 2005 the designers foretell these happenings:

Cars will fly. They'll become so light that they'll just float on a cushion of air a few inches off the ground, rather than roll on tires. Gas engines will become obsolete. Autos will have their own power plant, transforming sunlight into energy. Radar brakes will sense obstacles and stop the car or steer it away. Laser beams will guide you to your next destination, and even tell you when there is another vehicle in your path as far away as one mile. The ultimate will be a nuclear-powered car. It will run one year on a pellet dropped into the fuel tank.

While there have been other experimental cars conceived by Detroit companies since 1938, those described here represent the more interesting and exotic ones–and even some that are outlandish and garish.

1938
General Motors Y-Job

In 1938 General Motors Corp. originated the idea of a "dream" or experimental car to get public reaction to various design and engineering features it was working on. That year it introduced the famous Y-Job, a car which had many innovations ten years ahead of its time. The Y-Job was the first in a parade of experimental cars not only from GM, but from Ford and Chrysler–cars which were to excite millions of people in America and abroad. The Y-Job introduced the first power-drive convertible top and power windows in the industry and carried the fender-line through the front door. It also had the first concealed running board. After being shown across the country and tested extensively, it was retired to a GM warehouse. In 1964, it was brought out for public display once more when it was selected as one of America's twenty styling "milepost" cars for an exhibit at the New

York Automobile Show. Actually, it was not until thirteen years after its introduction–in 1951–that General Motors hatched its second and third experimental cars–the LeSabre and XP-300–and thus began an annual parade of futuristic cars which has not yet ended. Why the curious name "Y-Job"? According to General Motors Corp. designers, the letter "Y" was used originally to designate new experimental fighter planes being developed for World War II by the aircraft industry–for example, the "Y" P-40 fighter plane, which became the P-40 Warhawk, a famous plane of the Flying Tigers in Burma and China. Recalls one oldtime General Motors designer: "We picked up the letter "Y" for experimental cars, and it became a term of endearment in our design studios."

1 9 4 0
Chrysler Thunderbolt

Nicknamed "the push-button car" when exhibited in dealer showrooms, this two-passenger retractable hard-top coupe, designed and built by LeBaron, featured an automatic one-piece metal top that disappeared into a compartment behind the cockpit. Concealed head-lights, side windows, and deck lid were electrically con- trolled. Six Thunderbolts were built for display across the country, each painted and trimmed differently. Leather and Bedford cord upholstery was used. The instrument panel was leather-covered and had edge-lighted Lucite dials. Doors were push-button operated, from in- side and outside.

1940
Chrysler Newport

The body of this special phaeton was among the last designed and built in Detroit by LeBaron, a leading custom coachbuilding firm. Six were constructed, one of which served as Pace Car for the 1941 Indianapolis 500-Mile Race; the others were used in auto shows and for dealer showroom display. With the advanced (for 1940) envelope-type aluminum body, other design features were the dual cockpits with separate folding windshields, hydraulically controlled disappearing top, push-button door handles, and concealed headlights. The first Newport was painted bone white, with red leather interior trim. The chassis was that of a 1941 Chrysler Imperial.

1 9 5 0
Plymouth XX-500

The first Chrysler Corporation idea car designed and built by the Ghia firm in Turin, Italy, was constructed on a 1951 Plymouth chassis. Based on this example of hand craftsmanship, Ghia was awarded most of Chrysler's subsequent idea car commissions. The XX-500 was a simply styled four-door sedan upholstered in Bedford cord and leather. Body styling was typical of Italian contemporary special body design of that time.

1951
Chrysler K-310

The K-310 was a five-passenger sport coupe designed by Chrysler to combine American design tastes with European-inspired body styling. Features included large wire wheels, simulated spare tire mounting on deck lid, flush-mounted door handles, remote-controlled deck lid lock, and 1/3 - 2/3 split front seat back. The front seat base moved forward when the seat back was folded to provide extra rear seat entrance space. A unique counterbalanced mounting allowed the spare tire to be raised out of its trunk floor recess to a vertical position, for easy tire removal. This car was originally built on a standard 1951 Chrysler Saratoga chassis.

1 9 5 1
Buick LeSabre

The 1951 Buick LeSabre had a dual fuel system which used premium gas and methyl alcohol (methanol). The alcohol was injected into the combustion chambers through the carburetor at certain speeds for extra power boost. The fuel was stored in aircraft type 20 gallon rubberized fuel cells inside the twin tail fins–one for the gas and one for the alcohol. The car had the sweeping lines of a jet aircraft, and the grille resembled a jet pod. When the front lamps were turned on, the grille revolved out of sight and a pair of close-set headlamps, fitted on the reverse side, swung into place. Electric push-button door releases operated inside and out, and windows were lifted and lowered electrically. In the event of battery failure, door releases functioned mechanically with an extra push on the buttons or a turn of the car key. Instrument panel controls operated hydraulic jacks on each of the car's wheels. In the event of a blowout or flat tire, the driver could jack up the car without leaving his seat. An electrically driven screwjack, controlled by a switch, was available to adjust the driver's seat. One of the more unusual features was the electric convertible top. If the car was parked with the top open, rain falling on a sensitized spot between the seats actuated the top to close and raised the windows automatically.

1951
Buick XP-300

Considered super-streamlined for its day, the Buick XP-300 boasted an experimental supercharged V-8 engine weighing only 550 pounds but developing a tremendous 335 horsepower. It had two fuel tanks, one for methyl alcohol, the other for premium-grade gas. The tanks were behind the front seat. When operating at power outputs for ordinary driving, the engine operated an ordinary premium fuel. When the driver wanted a full-power burst, he depressed the accelerator past mid-position to open a second carburetor which fed the methyl alcohol into the combustion chamber. The car had a two-piece trunk lid which could be opened from either curb or street side. A tapered chrome fin extended down the center of the trunk from the rear window to the rear bumper, concealing the trunk hinges. The body was all aluminum. When the doors were closed, hydraulically operated steel bars slid into position, like the bolts of a bank vault. The hood could be raised or lowered hydraulically by an instrument panel control. Also, built-in automatic jacks permitted the driver to lift the car for a tire change by operating a control on the dashboard. Various aircraft-type gauges showed the driver everything he needed to know, including the horsepower the engine was developing, and even the oil level in the transmission, a unique feature at the time.

1 9 5 2
Chrysler C-200

Based on the styling profiles of the K-310–"blister" fender shapes, depressed belt line–the Chrysler C-200 was a five-passenger convertible coupe. Its chassis was a modified Chrysler New Yorker. Design features and basic car dimensions were similar to the K-310, including the special seat track and the spare tire stowage arrangement. The interior was upholstered in black leather, and the exterior was two-toned pale green with black. The "gun sight" taillight design was featured on later production Imperial models.

1 9 5 3
Chrysler Special

With elements of Continental sports car styling similar to the K-310 and C-200, this three-passenger sport coupe was first shown at the 1952 Paris Auto Show. Using a modified Chrysler New Yorker chassis, it featured a "fastback" roof line and knife-edge fender shapes. The grille frame and horizontal bumper bar appeared integral; vertical bumper guards formed the leading edges of the front fenders. A similar bumper treatment was used at the rear. The flush-mounted filler cap on the deck lid was push-button controlled by the driver, and the spare tire access door at the rear was hydraulically controlled. The body was metallic green with light green along the lower portion; the interior was upholstered in rich green leather. Originally, the exterior had a different two-tone combination. Racing knock-off-type wire wheels were used. Shown is the modified version, often called the "Thomas Special." Built in 1953 by Ghia for C.B. Thomas, then president of the Export Division of Chrysler Corporation, this car differed from the original special in grille outline molding, hood panel and cowl air intakes, door handles, and luggage compartment.

1953
Oldsmobile Starfire

The name "Starfire" was to become an Olds byword for at least ten years after this experimental model was introduced. It featured several innovations–panoramic windshields that extended around the door openings, spinner-type wheel discs, and a new low poised waist-high silhouette only 54.3 inches high with the top down. It had power brakes, power steering, and on the rear fenders power radio antennas. The low, sleek experimental prototype was named after Lockheed's F-94B Starfire all-weather fighter, then being supplied to the Air Force. This prototype presaged several ideas that were to reach production shortly. Its fiberglass body was among the earliest of that type; its practicality would be proven in volume production by the Corvette, and later the Avanti. Many Starfire features, particularly the large oval grille, would be standard in 1956, but perhaps most remarkable was its overall concept–a sporty personal car with six-passenger capacity, an idea that would become one of America's favorites, exemplified by the 1958 Thunderbird and the 1962 Studebaker Gran Turismo Hawk, plus many sporty cars, including Oldsmobile's production Starfires of the Sixties. The fiberglass reinforced plastic body of the experimental Starfire was finished in regal turquoise with white and turquoise leather upholstery. The safety padded instrument panel had five gauges spaced between the speedometer and the radioe speaker. Front seat backs were framed with chrome bands, and the Orlon top lowered into a recess having a metal ribbed cover. Dual backup lights, and exhaust ports were integral with the end bumper guards.

1 9 5 3
De Soto Adventurer I

Despite its close-coupled silhouette, the Adventurer I was a four-passenger, high-performance sport coupe with many 1953 De Soto chassis components. Short body overhang, full wheel openings, exposed dual exhaust system, and long, flat hood exemplified the sports car look. Satin-finish aluminum formed the background for the instrument cluster of circular dials. The rear deck had a large racing-type fuel filler in the center and a spare tire stowage compartment below. The exterior was off-white; the interior, black leather with white piping.

1 9 5 3
Chrysler D'Elegance

A three-passenger sport coupe using a shortened Chrysler New Yorker chassis, D'Elegance combined advanced body design with several driver-passenger conveniences: matching luggage to fit the carpeted compartment behind the seat and covered in the same black-and-yellow, hand-sewn leather used for the seats and door panels; a novel fold-up center armrest in the seat cushion; black leather-covered instrument panel; and a unique spare tire mounting. An electro-hydraulic mechanism raised the spare tire out of its recess in the rear deck and downward, for easy removal from its mounting. The body exterior was painted metallic red. Note the "gun sight" taillights similar to those later used for the Imperial.

1 9 5 3
Buick Wildcat

This experimental car was designed and built primarily to test the use of fiberglass in automobile body building. Characteristic Buick fenderports (one of Buick's most notable design features in the early days) were placed on top of the fenders rather than at the sides for cooling. A unique feature of the Wildcat was the "roto-static" front wheel discs which remained stationary while the wheels revolved about them. Two air inlets, one on each side of the hood ornament, were incorporated in the hood for better carburation. The front bumper and grille frame were a single unit. The grille bars were mounted in the frame vertically and were of concave design for better protection. Two pointed bumper "bombs" projected from the grille for added protection. The one-piece windshield was a wraparound type with a 60-degree slope to the rear. The rear fenders had vertical louvers at the wheel housings to exhaust tire and brake heat. The windows, top, and seat were operated hydraulically, and when the top was down it recessed into the body of the car with a special panel covering it, eliminating the necessity of a boot.

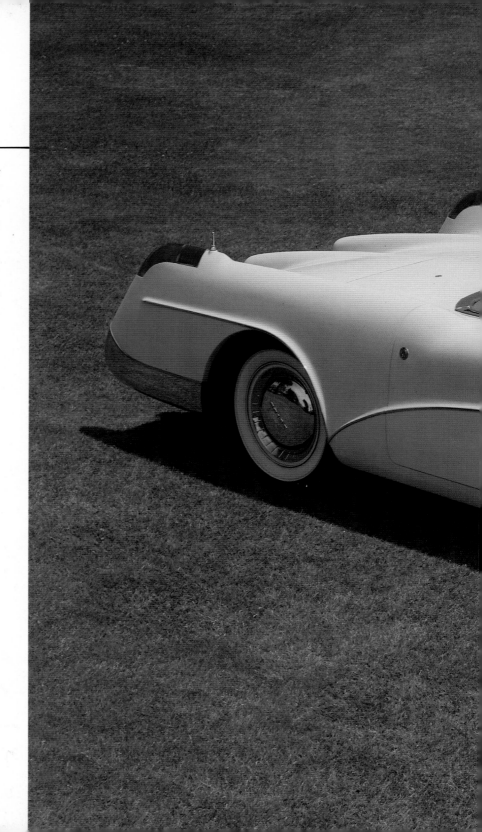

1953
Ford XL-500

This was one of the few experimental cars that had push buttons for the automatic transmission, mounted vertically in the center of the steering wheel. It had a fiberglass body and a tinted all-glass roof supported by narrow posts and a wide overhead sash. Arched rear fender lines were reminiscent of high-speed record cars driven by John Cobb, Goldie Gardner, and others in those years. There was a suggestion of fins on the rear fenders. Vertical bumpers were integrated with taillight assemblies, and a horizontal bumper bar protruded from the bottom of the trunk. Besides the conventional instrument panel, which included a 150 mph speedometer, there was a "magic eye" fuel gauge and an auxiliary panel in the windshield header bar. Designed to shorten the driver's eye travel from the road to the panel, it insured prompt warning in case of any low instrument readings. In the event of a flat tire, the car had automatic jacks which lifted it. The XL-500 was equipped with a telephone and dictaphone. When the telephone receiver was lifted, the antenna at the top of the windshield was automatically energized and swung from its horizontal position to a vertical position. The car included a foot treadle for horn operation. Throttle-type controls for air conditioning, lights, wipers, and other gauges were located on a center pedestal.

1 9 5 4
Oldsmobile Cutlass

The Cutlass had no outside trunk lid to open. Access to the luggage compartment was reached from inside the car. The rear window featured an unusual glass treatment. There were louvers on the surface of the pane of glass, giving a Venetian blind effect but allowing full visibility through the rear-view mirror. Instrumentation of the Cutlass was the "competition-type," resembling aircraft instruments. Rather than being located across the dash-board in conventional style, the instruments started at the center of the dash panel, extended vertically to the floor, and then were placed along the transmission tunnel, dividing the seat compartment. The underside of the front fenders—or wheel housings—was wide open, finished in paint throughout, and was perforated to permit exhaust of engine heat. High fins ran the length of each

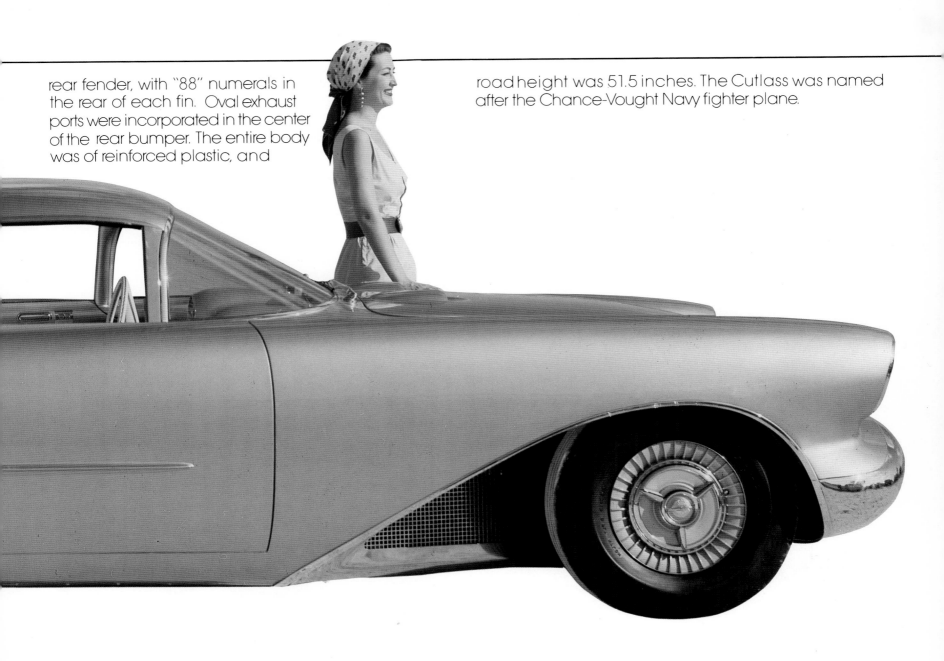

rear fender, with "88" numerals in
the rear of each fin. Oval exhaust
ports were incorporated in the center
of the rear bumper. The entire body
was of reinforced plastic, and

road height was 51.5 inches. The Cutlass was named
after the Chance-Vought Navy fighter plane.

1 9 5 4
De Soto Adventurer II

Although larger than its four-passenger predecessor, this two-passenger sport coupe was one of the most aerodynamic idea cars. With a 1954 De Soto chassis, the car featured rounded lower body shapes as viewed from front or rear–and a dramatic sloping contour joining the lower body to the roof. An unusual front end effect was created by a honeycomb-textured grille and surrounding sculptured sheet metal; the front bumper was abandoned. The large tinted plastic rear window was power-retractable into the rear deck area. Trimmed in black and white cowhide, the interior featured a control console between seats and instrument panel covered with non-reflective black leather. The body was painted red.

1954
Plymouth Explorer

The Explorer was a smoothly styled two-passenger sport coupe built on a conventional 1954 Plymouth chassis. The body design was based on the use of sculptured sheet metal, with a minimum of bright trim. Horizontal side moldings were painted ivory to contrast with the bright metallic green body color, and the bucket seats were done in white leather with black accents. Exhaust pipes were integrated with the taillights. Custom features of the interior included two leather-trimmed storage compartments and a carpeted luggage space behind the seats, with two matched suitcases. Unusual retractable radio tuner controls were concealed by a movable instrument panel section.

1 9 5 4
Chevrolet Nomad

A Corvette station wagon? You say you never heard of one? Take a look at the pictures. One is a concept 1954 Corvette with a station wagon roof on it; the other is the original Vette, which made its debut in June, 1953, as a soft-top convertible. Notice that the front end on both models is almost identical, with the sloping hood and slotted vertical grille. Pieces of the 1954 concept "Corvette Station Wagon" were actually put into production in 1955, and the car became the Chevrolet Bel Air Nomad wagon. Today, the Nomad is a collector's item. Before the 1950s, station wagons weren't very much in demand because many had body sides made of wood, which deteriorated. But the 50s started the boom for such family vehicles, and Chevrolet jumped right into the market with the Nomad "Corvette." Chevrolet liked the name Nomad because it connoted "roaming, a wanderer." One popular automotive publication referred to it as the "world's greatest station wagon." However, it didn't last long. Production of the Nomad was halted in 1957 because of its high price, which detracted buyers. For an extra $350 one could buy a sporty Corvette.

1954
Dodge Firearrow Roadster I

The Firearrow I was an experimental roadster body mock-up on a conventional 1954 Dodge chassis. Its overall width was more than twice the maximum body height at the cowl. The only exterior bright trim areas were the grille scoop insert, name plates, exposed exhaust pipes, and lower deck at rear. Otherwise, the body was free of applied ornamentation. The side molding encircling the body was painted a metallic gray, contrasted with the bright metallic red body color. Yellow-buff leather accented with maroon piping covered the deeply padded seats. Other features included one-piece unframed tempered glass windshield, racing-type steering wheel with polished natural wood rim, and dual headlights–which have since become an industry standard.

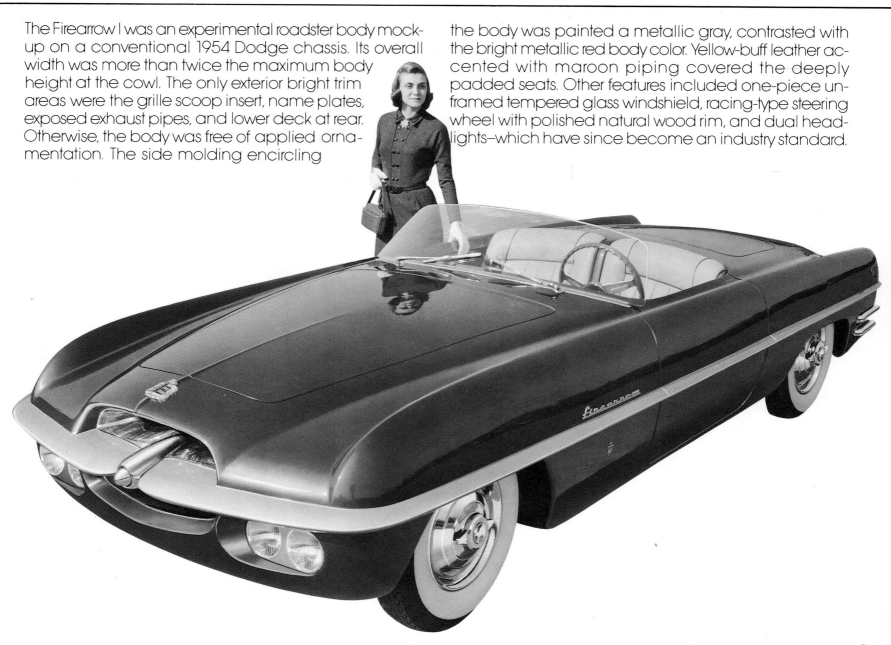

1 9 5 4
Dodge Firearrow Roadster II

Modified slightly from the original roadster, this car had a 119-in. wheelbase and production chrome-plated wire wheels. While the basic body shape was identical, single headlamps were faired into pods at "corners" of front end sheet metal to break the body side molding at the front. The grille scoop also was restyled, as were the taillights. The gearshift lever was mounted on the steering column rather than on the floor tunnel, as in the original roadster. Body color was pale yellow, with a black central bar through the grille and black body side molding. The interior was finished in saddle-grain black leather. A compartment behind the cockpit was for luggage, and the rearmost compartment for spare tire stowage.

1 9 5 4
Dodge Firearrow Sport Coupe

While apparently similar to the Firearrow roadster, this two-seat high-performance coupe had distinctive upper-structure, front end and rear end styling. The concave grille was flanked by dual headlamps, and short vertical "bumperettes" provided the only bumper protection, front and rear. The chassis was basically that of a 1954 Dodge. The exterior was metallic blue with gray full-length body side molding; the interior was of medium-blue leather with white pleated leather seat inserts and accents. A large parcel bin and ash recever were located in a console between the bucket seats. This car attained 143.44 mph on the high-speed test track at Chrysler Proving Grounds, in a Closed-Course World's Record (for women) by Betty Skelton. For this event, the engine was specially modified.

1954
Dodge Firearrow Convertible

This was the last of four separate Dodge Firearrow idea cars constructed by Ghia. Very similar in exterior body and mechanical details to the sport coupe, this four-passenger convertible coupe featured a bold quilted-pattern all-leather interior in black and white. The bucket seats were individually adjustable, and seat backs could be reclined. Rear seats were removable to expose a mahogany luggage platform with chrome skid strips. A dome lamp was located in the heavily padded and lined convertible top. Body paint was bright red. This car inspired the limited-production Dual-Ghia cars produced by Dual Motors, Inc., in Detroit.

1 9 5 4
Buick Wildcat II

Its revolutionary front-end design had "flying-wing" front fenders that flared straight out from the body, exposing the entire front wheel well and part of the front-end suspension, which was chrome plated. A rakish sports convertible, Wildcat II had a fiberglass body. Free-standing headlamps were mounted on the cowl with parking and directional signal lights on the front end underneath the fender shroud. Bumpers were shaped with two big torpedo-like guards, known in those days as "Dagmar" bumper guards, a name taken after a contemporary sexy celebrity with a good-sized bosom. The car had two huge spotlights, one on either side of the windshield, an accessory that was very much in vogue in those days. Wildcat featured Buick's traditional portholes, but they were made larger and placed on the top of the fenders instead of the sides as was customary. (Such portholes were Buick's trademark for years.) The car was only 35.3 inches high at the front cowl.

1 9 5 4
Ford FX Atmos

Designers of the 1950s must have had a penchant for high shark-like tail fins. Not only did this experimental car sport fins, but it also had two extremely sharp "spears"-like aerials–protruding from the front fenders. These, it was explained, could be used for controlling the vehicle by radio and keeping it from running into other vehicles. (Nothing was explained as to what these might do to pedestrians.) Ford said that the "FX" stood for "future experimental" and that the name "Atmos" had been taken from "atmosphere," which Ford said came from "free and unlimited creative thinking." The Atmos had no engine. It was a three-passenger model with a "bubble"

top The driver sat in a central seat and would steer the vehicle with hand grips located at elbow level. The hand grips also controlled other functions. Two other passengers could sit slightly to the rear of the driver on each side. Within the driver's cockpit was a radar screen. At the time, stylists were not clear as to whether this would be used for viewing television, airplanes and rockets, or other cars on the highway miles away. Stylists did point out that at that time a system had already been devised for controlling driverless automobiles on highways which would be wired and would throw out electrical control impulses.

1954
Oldsmobile F-88

This rakish low-slung, open sports car had no interior door handles. You simply pressed a button in the upper center of the door to open it. The F-88 was a two-passenger model with recessed sports car-type seats. It had the Oldsmobile panoramic windshield, a honeycomb-type grille set in an oval between the upper and lower bumper bars, and jet airfoil wheel disks that gave a turbine affect. Instrumentation was the "competition-type", resembling aircraft instruments. Rather than being located across the dashboard in conventional style, the instruments started at the center of the dash panel, extended vertically to the floor, and then were placed along the transmission tunnel, dividing the seat compartment. The F-88 was powered by a 250-horsepower advanced version of the "Rocket" engine. Displacement was 324 cu. in. The F-88 had a wheelbase of 102 inches and overall length of 167½ inches. Height with the top down at the windshield was only 48 inches. The upholstery and steering wheel were finished in pigskin. Exhaust stacks were integral with the lower rear fenders in oval openings, with decorative louvers just ahead of them on the fender panel. Seven vertical bumper guards were part of the rear bumper, whose center section dropped down to reveal a horizontal compartment for the spare tire. Rollers made it easy to remove the spare tire. There were two cowl ventilators and also an air scoop in the middle of the hood to provide air for the carburetor. The license plate was recessed in the rear deck. A large cap for the gasoline tank was situated behind the seat.

1 9 5 4
Firebird I

This was probably the most advanced car designed by General Motors in 1954. There were actually three Firebirds built. The Firebird I was the first car ever designed around a single stick control system which eliminated the conventional steering wheel, brake pedal, and accelerator. You simply pushed the stick forward to accelerate. Moving it to left or right steered it in those directions, and pulling back on the handle applied the brakes. The control stick was located in the center, so that either the driver or passenger could operate the car. A two-passenger gas turbine-powered car, the Firebird resembled a modern-day jet plane, with a pointed nose, high dorsal fin at the tail, and plastic bubble canopy like the cockpit of an aircraft. The car had a 110-volt generator which provided 60-cycle electrical power. With this, you could plug into the car for power to run household appliances if your home electrical power went out. Other novel features of the Firebird included special drag brakes at the reat which opened like the jaws of an alligator to help slow the car down, a lighting system that turned an automatically when it got dark, an ultrasonic key which opened the doors by high frequency sound waves from as much as fifteen feet away; and a timer which you could preset to start the car before you entered it.

1 9 5 4
Plymouth Belmont

Built as a styling experiment on a 1954 Dodge chassis, the body of this two-passenger sports car was made of reinforced fiberglass by Briggs Manufacturing Company for Chrysler Corporation. The car was used for publicity purposes by the Plymouth Division. Finished in light metallic blue, it had little ornamentation. Radio and power antenna controls were located in the center armrest between the white leather bucket seats, and a luggage compartment was provided behind the cockpit. A removable fabric top and the spare tire were stored in a separate trunk.

1955
Oldsmobile Delta

This experimental car featured an aluminum roof, dual fuel tanks, and swivel seats. Oldsmobile called it a "four-passenger close coupled coupe." The Delta was styled with unusually large front wheel openings with an oval contour. A chrome side moulding originated on the front fender just behind the headlights, dipped to a lower plane on the door, and then merged with the rear bumper blade. This moulding served as color separation for the two-tone paint effect. The belt line was lowered between the panoramic windshield and the rear window to accentuate the car's streamlined appearance. The body, except the roof, was made of fiberglass. The hood treatment of the Delta was unusual in that the hood extended laterally from one front fender crown to the other. A chrome cove on each fender crown hid the hood edge, but the entire hood could be raised to reveal the 250-h.p. "Rocket" engine with 10 to 1 compression ratio. Windshield and window glass in the Delta was tinted light blue to harmonize with the overall color and also to protect the passengers from strong sunlight. Two-tone blue leather upholstery and blue anodized aluminum marked the interior. Entry to the rear seats through the wide door of the Delta was made easier by the individualized front seats that swiveled and also folded and moved forward in a single operation.

1955
Chrysler
Flight-Sweep I

This car, together with its sister idea cars, Flight Sweep II and Falcon, promoted the Chrysler Corporation's "Forward Look" theme of the mid-50s. Styling features of this four-passenger sport convertible included clamshell-type front fenders, sweeping body character line, finned rear fenders, and wheel covers simulating exposed brake drum and cooling fins. An "inner" deck lid held the spare tire; and the outer deck lid, the tire cover. The body was finished in white and bronze, with harmonizing leather interior trim. Large circular dials and toggle-type controls were featured in the instrument panel; heater, turn signals, transmission gear selector and radio controls were located in a console between the front seats. The chassis was a modified 1954 De Soto.

1 9 5 5
Chrysler
Flight-Sweep II

The same basic body forms were used for this four-passenger hardtop coupe as for the Flight-Sweep I, except for the roof and upperstructure. Front fenders, cowl, and body were welded integrally with the frame and, as was common practice in all Ghia-built special bodies, all exposed body joints were metal-finished for a smooth surface appearance. Exterior and interior trim also was identical with the convertible, though color combinations differed. Exterior paint was medium green and black. The interior featured green and black patent leather seats and perforated vinyl headlining. The Flight-Sweep models and Falcon were displayed in many cities across the country during 1955 and 1956, exemplifying Chrysler's "Forward Look" theme.

1 9 5 5
Buick Wildcat III

Made of reinforced fiberglass, this four-passenger model was dubbed the "toy convertible" by Buick designers. For a so-called toy car, it certainly had a super powerful V-8 engine, which jetted out 280 horsepower and carried four carburetors, much more than any modern U.S.-made car. Even the largest 1990 Buick fires out a mere 165 h.p. The rear end design of the Wildcat could have been mistaken for the front end. There were two bomb-shaped rear bumpers on either side, and the downward curving trunk area resembled a front grille design. Front parking and directional signals were housed in two additional bumper bombs. The grillework was of a fine screen material. The Wildcat was painted a flashy "Kimberly" red, so named in honor of Jim Kimberly, famous sports car racer. Overall length of the Wildcat was 190 inches, which was probably considered small in those days of behemoth cars. That's about the length of Buick's longest standard cars today.

1 9 5 5
Lincoln Futura

One of the more spectacular and revolutionary concept cars of the 1950s was the Lincoln Futura–so spectacular that it caught the interest of Hollywood producers, who later acquired it for filming the highly-popular "Batman" television series, which aired on ABC from 1966 to 1968. The studio converted the car and renamed it "Batmobile." Built at an original cost of $250,000 by Ford Motor Co., it was a true "laboratory on wheels." With "sharkfin" front and rear fenders, the Futura was a sleek low-slung model with a twin Plexiglas dome and resembled a jet racing boat more than an automobile. It was 19 feet long and only 52.8 inches high. The twin domes, set over two bucket-type seats, were pivoted by concealed exterior door handles to admit driver and passenger. There were no windows to open or close. Special intake and exhaust louvers behind the seats provided air for comfort. Powered by a 300 horsepower V-8 engine, the Futura had a push-button Turbo-Drive automatic transmission with controls on a center pedestal armrest. An electronic safety device prevented the car from starting with the top up or doors open. The car featured a central instrument cluster with all the gauges in the steering column binnacle. The steering wheel itself revolved around the binnacle. There was a circular radio antenna mounted on the trunk. It was combined with an "audio approach" microphone which picked up and amplified the sounds of a car approaching from the rear.

1955
Chevrolet Biscayne

With a grille resembling giant shark teeth, the Biscayne had what Chevrolet called a "stratospheric" windshield for maximum visibility. It curved into the roof. Two huge headlamps were mounted on the hood. It was considered a new concept at that time to round out the back fenders for a "simple aerodynamic form to completely eliminate fenders". The tips of the front fenders housed parking lamps which were larger than the headlamps, and there were air scoops integrated within the bezel to cool brakes. The sculptured side body panels were clean, without any mouldings. Front seats pivoted for easy entrance and exit. The seat cushions and back were suspended in a thin chrome airfoil frame with thin sponge crash surfaces along the rear edges.

1 9 5 5
Chrysler Falcon

This competition-type sport roadster culminated a design study by Chrysler Corporation's Advance Styling Studio. The body was of unit construction with an integral cellular platform frame structure and was nearly identical to two previously built Falcon roadsters. A bold grid-type grille, recessed headlamps, a long and plain hood line, and externally mounted dual exhaust pipes combined the advanced and traditional in appearance. The manually operated convertible top was stored behind the seat under a folding lid. Exterior paint was black. The interior featured red leather with ivory leather accents and toggle-type instrument controls.

1955
Ford Mystere

This car had one of the most unusual windshield treatments. The front glass curved all around to the vertical center pillar at the back of the door, and the entire glass lifted up. There were no sliding or roll-down windows. Passengers rellied on the air conditioner for air. What looked like a periscope in the upper center of the windshield was a roof vent. There were huge round taillamps beneath the rear fender fins. Where parking lamps are usually located in front there were protruding bumper pods for air cooler reservoirs. The Mystere carried a gas turbine engine mounted in the rear, which was cooled by large air intake scoops at the front of the rear fenders. The steering wheel was similar to a control stick in an airplane and could be swung from the driver's side to the front passenger.

1 9 5 6
Mercury XM Turnpike Cruiser

One of the unique features of this car was the huge eye-catching concave channels moulded into the rear fenders, a design which extended into the front doors. This treatment terminated at the rear into two enormous V-shaped taillamps. The channels were outlined in chrome. The car had an extremely low silhouette (only 4.4 feet high), and featured virtually unobstructed vision in every direction. Side windows extended along the entire side and wrapped fully around the corners at the rear.

The windshield wrapped up into the roof. The only roof supports were narrow chrome pillars at the windshield and similar ones inboard at the rear. The rear window could be opened electrically. To prevent head bumping in this low car, part of the glass roof over the doors opened upward automatically when the doors were opened. The front end featured jet-pod twin bumpers, one under each headlamp.

1 9 5 6
Chrysler Plainsman

The Plainsman was an advance-design station wagon with several features later used on production models, such as folding rearward-facing third seat, roll-down rear window–both electrically controlled from the front compartment or at the rear. With second and third seats folded, a flat carpeted cargo floor was provided. Steps for third seat entry were hydraulically retracted into rear bumper slots. A spare tire was mounted behind the left taillight. Brown-and-white unborn calfskin upholstery contrasted with the high-metallic beige exterior paint. Other features were individually adjustable front seat backs and passenger air intake in the "stepped" roof. The roof was covered with off-white vinyl fabric.

1 9 5 6
Chrysler Norseman

The Chrysler Norseman—with radical styling departure—was being shipped from Italy on July 26, 1956, aboard the Italian liner Andrea Doria, but was lost when the ship sank in some 200 feet of water. Designed by Ghia of Turin, Italy, it featured more structural, chassis, electrical, and styling innovations than any other experimental car ever designed by the company. Although the car was intended to have as great structural strength as today's automobiles, it had no posts or pillars to support the roof. Support was accomplished by means of structural cantilever arches which curved upward from the rear of the frame and over the passenger compartment of the car. Glass surrounding the passenger compartment was uninterrupted, with the exception of the two arches of steel curving upward in the rear. In addition, there was a 12-square-foot panel of glass in the roof that was power-operated and slid forward, leaving the roof over the rear seat area open. All major body panels on the car were made of aluminum. The Norseman had a sharply sloping hood, upswept tail fins, and a covered, smooth underbody for aerodynamic efficiency.

1 9 5 6
Oldsmobile Golden Rocket

The huge bumper guards at the back of the two rear fenders resembled rocket launchers. The extension of this form was carried throughout the entire length of the body, giving an overall rocket effect. The two front headlamps also resembled smaller rockets. Even the grille was projectile-shaped and was made of air-filled rubber. This two-passenger model was made of reinforced plastic and finished in gold. The hood was like a supersonic aircraft in its streamlined dimensions, and the passenger compartment was like a jet plane's bubble canopy. As either door opened, the roof panel automatically raised and the seat rose three inches and swiveled

outwards for easy entry or exit. Plastic dorsal fins just to the rear of the doors on the fender crown line were lighted in red and served as running lights. The speedometer was on the hub of the steering wheel, which had only two spokes, serving as a radius on which to tilt it forward when entering or leaving the car. An unusual feature was the location of the louvers in the rear of the passenger compartment, permitting air to exhaust from the compartment when the fresh air inlets in the hood were opened. The Rocket was powered by a 275-h.p. "Rocket" engine with 9.1 to 1 compression ratio. Road height was a mere 49½ inches.

1 9 5 6
Dodge Dart

Ink blots, driven by 200-mile-per-hour winds, helped to shape Chrysler's most revolutionary car of the 1950s–the Dart. The ink blot tests, conducted in one of Europe's largest wind tunnels, enabled engineers to design the Dart to pierce the air with the least possible air disturbance and still provide comfort for four passengers. As a result, the Dart was the most nearly perfect aerodynamic passenger car design in the world at the time. Its aerodynamic purity gave it less than one-third the air drag of any other passenger car then built. The engine compartment was uniquely designed to neutralize the force of the air entering the compartment, thus eliminating upward pull or downward drag of the air. Thus, stability was at a maximum and drag at a minimum. Other Dart innovations for the time included a three-dimensional windshield, sloping at a sharper angle and offering more visibility than any windshield in production. The windshield wrapped into the roof as well as around the sides. Full-wrap, rubber-mounted bumpers provided complete protection around the car body, yet blended into the car so aerodynamically that they seemed a part of the car body. A sliding roof panel telescoped into a concealed compartment behind the rear seat. The roof could also be partially retracted so as to leave the front seat open and rear seat covered.

1 9 5 6
General Motors XP-500

The XP-500 was the world's first automobile with a free piston engine. The engine could burn animal, vegetable, or mineral oils, and pump hot gasses through a pipe to a turbine which drove the rear wheels. The engine, which developed 250 horsepower, consisted of two parallel cylinders, each containing a set of two horizontally opposed pistons. Compared with a conventional auto piston engine, it had few high precision parts. Therefore, it operated virtually without vibration, and the comparative absence of rotating parts caused little wear of rubbing parts. An air-fuel charge fired between the pistons with injectors similar to those used in diesels. The compressed air bounced the pistons back toward inner "dead center," and as they travelled inward they also compressed air that pumped into a diesel cylinder. The back-and-forth movement continued to compress air, which was piped to a turbine. A pipe to the turbine ran along one side of the chassis frame, thus giving the passenger compartment a "flat floor." The XP-500 had a rounded all-glass roof, and the hood sloped down in one line from the windshield to the low horizontal grille opening. The rear fenders were arched over the wheels, like a bird's wings. Further development work on the free piston car was stopped within three years because the company had other more promising projects in the works. The engine was also somewhat too noisy.

1 9 5 6
Firebird II

Like Firebird I, the Firebird II was a gas turbine car. It was constructed from titanium, a lightweight metal of great strength, which is non-corrosive and immune to salt water and marine atmosphere. Resembling a shark at the rear end, Firebird II was designed for adaptability to use on an electronic highway of the future. By means of a television screen on the dashboard, the driver would make contact with an operator in a control tower along the "Safety Highway." The operator would guide the driver into a high speed lane with a metallic strip in its center.

Once the electronic coils in the cones in the front end of the Firebird II established contact with the "beam" in the metallic strip, the car would be automatically controlled by the tower operator. The driver would then fold the steering posts forward and enjoy the ride. Unlike conventional cars, engine exhaust gases rose vertically from ports atop the rear fenders. The luggage compartment deck and floor lifted automatically, bringing the floor up to the height of a person's waist for easy loading.

1 9 5 6
Buick Centurion

The rear end of this car resembled the tail cone of a jet plane, with all lines tapering in toward a single focal point. There was a "seeing eye" television camera pointing out through the cone, transmitting the rear view to a 4-by-6-inch screen on the instrument panel and eliminating the traditional mirror. The camera was equipped with a specially designed wide-angle lens, which presented a wider vision of what was behind the car than the conventional rear-view mirror. It picked up a view as far back as the naked eye could see. The shockproof mounting of this camera and tube unit prevented any

disturbance in the picture's clarity as the car rode over bumps. The front end of the Centurion was of a revolutionary new design with the long hood sloping toward the front and the grille and headlights recessed well behind the bumper, which was an integral part of the body shell. The top half of the car was all glass, with just a few thin steel struts to provide proper rigidity.

1 9 5 6
Pontiac Club de Mer

This true sports car had not only a tall tail fin resembling a shark but a front end that looked like a shark's mouth, slightly open. It had two individual curved windshields, or windscreens, and was designed both as an all-around sports car or for competition racing. The Club de Mer used hand-formed aluminum body panels with highly sculptured rounded contours. The car was long and low. It stretched 180 inches and stood only 38.4 inches high. Side trim was minimal, consisting of three bright metal stars behind the front wheel openings and three chrome strips highlighting the wind splits molded into the door.

The hood swept all the way down the nose, along with two wide chrome strips. The transmission was mounted just aft of the passenger compartment to insure proper weight distribution. One of the car's most interesting features was the unique front end design, with no headlights visible. Headlights were located in the back of the nose section. When the lights were turned on, the entire section revolved to expose the headlamps in proper driving position. All controls were mounted either in the center armrest or at the side rest in the driver's door.

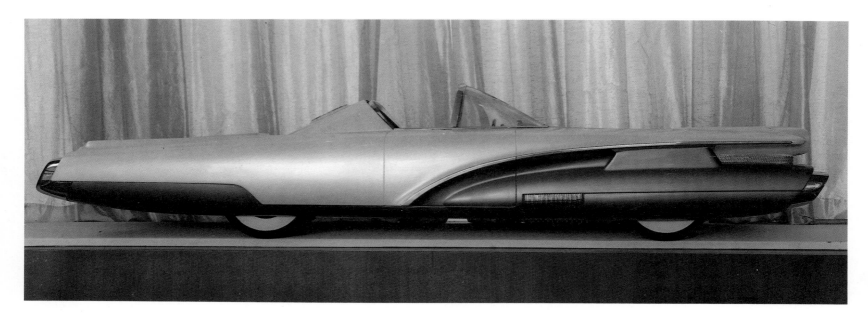

1 9 5 7
Ford X-1000

This car resembled a cigar. It was designed to carry the engine at either the front or the rear end. The driver's seat was positioned in front of two passenger seats. A built-in television, hi-fi, and retractable safety chest bar were included for passengers. The car had an aircraft-type bubble canopy, suspended fins, and fenders with highlights designed aerodynamically into the fender surfaces. The canopy retracted to make the car a convertible, and the rear fins gave directional stability. The X-1000 was designed to accommodate any of several possible power plants, including present piston engine, a gas turbine, or a free-piston. Air-cooled oil coolers were mounted on the front fenders, and a similarly exposed after-cooler was atop the rear. Torpedo-shaped taillights were mounted inside the tail fins. The taillights could enclose radar devices to warn of approaching vehicles through flashing lights on the instrument panel. An exhaust diffuser was mounted in the rear center to minimize exhaust temperature and noise. The instrument panel and a push-button transmission were unique. They were suspended in the center of a deep-dish steering wheel. Three seats were arranged in a triangular pattern, with the driver in the center front and two passengers rearward at his sides.

1 9 5 8
Ford La Galaxie

In the La Galaxie there were three individually adjustable seats in the front. The rear was spacious enough for three more adults, who sat in "Form-Flow" seats that were integrated with the side panels. There was only one big wide door on each side of this "sedan." The huge windshield extended over the car's top and swept back over the passenger compartment. La Galaxie's butterfly roof opened outward from the middle to permit easy entrance and exit. The two headlamp bezels were almost as large as those on a locomotive and incorporated fluorescent lighting. The car's upper all-transparent structure had a unique looping-curve rear side window set into an almost blind quarter panel. The rear window slanted inward sharply at the bottom. The car's shrouded look offered a marked departure from the appearance of contemporary American cars. Normal offsets between glass and sheet metal areas were eliminated so that all window glass was nearly flush with the sides of the car and its roof. Transmission and turn signal controls were on the steering wheel, which seemed to literally "grow" out of the left pod. Fine-textured grillework ran along the sides from the bottom of the headlights to the middle of the door and served as exhaust ports for the engine. Most of the rear end design was taken up by two giant chrome-lined oval areas that housed massive taillights. The trunk lid was made of two pieces, permitting loading from street or curb side. The car had a "proximity" device which electrically slowed or stopped it if some object came in its path.

1 9 5 8
XP-700 Corvette

There were no front bumpers on this experimental Corvette, which today would be against U.S. Government regulations. Instead, the car had a "floating oval-shaped grille," with broad frontal air scoops underneath. The low hood overhang of the fiberglass body, snubbed rear fenders, and transparent canopy imparted a flavor of the most advanced sports car. The special bubble-top treatment was said to eliminate glare completely, and there was a periscope-type rear-view mirror on the roof to provide an unobstructed view of the road behind. Fenders had air scoops on the sides for added brake cooling.

1958
Plymouth Cabana

Three design objectives were achieved in this four-door hardtop station wagon: (1) to combine all desirable station wagon convenience features in one original body mock-up, (2) to design for ambulance or hearse conversion; and (3) to reduce the boxy squared-off rear end appearance of contemporary station wagons. Second and third seats and the passenger portion of the front seat folded into floor wells to allow a flat carpeted cargo floor from front toeboard to tail gate. A short floor-height center pillar and center-locking doors allowed maximum side-loading accessibility. The full-width side-opening rear door was power-hinged for easy cargo loading and passenger entry into the third seat. Two sliding clear-plastic rear roof panel sections also aided third seat entry and improved usable cargo height. The interior was trimmed in green metallic leather to match the metallic green exterior. The Cabana was built by Ghia on a 1958 Plymouth chassis, less engine and drive line.

1 9 5 8
Chrysler Imperial D'Elegance

Proportional emphasis on the front end and fastback roof and deck shape were featured on this four-door hardtop body mock-up. The chassis was that of a 1958 Imperial, less engine and drive line. Some of the sculptured sheet-metal contours of this body inspired the styling of later Chrysler Corporation production cars—the squared front fender eyebrows, canted rear fender fin faired into the rear door, and pod-type housings for taillights. Other features included special door handles and window linkage for side windows, which were nearly flush with outer door panels; concealed head lamps; and "square"-shaped steering wheel. The exterior was finished in metallic blue, and the cloth and metallic leather interior was rich medium blue, with finely pleated seat bolsters.

1 9 5 8
Ford Nucleon

What looked like an ornamental spare tire on the trunk was really an atomic core in a reactor at the rear of the car. The odd-looking vehicle was named the Nucleon, providing a glimpse into an atomic-powered future when drivers would be able to select their own horsepower. The car would be controlled at the driver's whim, much as the intensity of the reaction in a nuclear pile is controlled. Depending upon the size of their core, cars like the Nucleon might be capable of traveling 5,000 miles or more without recharging. They would be recharged at special facilities similar to present-day service stations. The drive train itself was part of the lower package, and electronic torque converters might take the place of the drive train now used. There were twin shark-like rear fender fins, and slit beam horizontal headlights up front. Retractable front and rear bumpers provided added aerodymamic advantages. The front wheels were behind the driver's cockpit, giving rise to the premise that any likely atomic car would be extremely heavy, hence the axle positions. Although atomic-powered cars are not practical at the moment, it is conceivable that new developments in metallurgy and other branches of science might eventually bring them to realization. The Nucleon was designed with the assumption that the present bulkiness and weight of their nuclear reactors and their attendant shielding will someday be reduced.

1 9 5 8
Ford Volante

Although the day when there will be an aero-car in every garage is still far off, the Volante indicated one direction that the styling of such a vehicle could take. The car might be powered by means of three units arranged in a triangular pattern, which would provide both lift and thrust. The forward unit was composed of two counter-rotating blades and a motor, while each of the two rear units was made up of a single set of blades moving in opposite directions to offset torque.

1 9 5 8
Firebird III

General Motors' experimental Firebird III was the first space-age inspired car. Beneath its missile-like shape, the tools of the space-age—transistors, computers, and electronics—were employed for the first time to give automatic guidance and improved passenger comfort to automobiles. Firebird III was the first car ever designed around a single stick control system to eliminate the conventional steering wheel, brake pedal, and accelerator. The first Firebird, a single-seat car, introduced at the GM Motorama of 1954, was the first gas turbine-powered automobile built and tested in the United States. Firebird II, a four-passenger car introduced at the Motorama of 1956, carried forward gas turbine progress and featured significant advances in passenger comfort. The second Firebird also presented a concept of a car under automatic guidance on an electronically-controlled highway of tomorrow. Firebird III carried this concept into reality. Through electronic "sniffers" located beneath the car, it could follow low-frequency power in a cable in the highway to automatically guide the car. It had a fiberglass body and was pearlescent silver-gold in color. The car measured 44.8 inches at the top of the bubbles and 57.3 inches at the tip of the dorsal fin. Firebird III had two engines—a 225 horsepower Whirlfire gas turbine engine located in the rear and a 10 horsepower aluminum engine located in the nose which drove all the accessories. Featuring the most advanced passenger compartment design of its day, the car had the first single-dial electronic temperature system. Through electronics it could maintain a single temperature setting even if the car were driven from the North Pole to the Equator. Large gull-wing doors swung diagonally up to offer effortless passenger entry. Other features included a lighting system that turned on automatically when daylight turned to darkness, an "ultra-sonic key" which opened the doors by high frequency sound waves, and a timer which could be set to start the accessory drive engine prior to passenger entry to precondition the temperature.

1959
Cadillac Cyclone

Equipped with radar in two large nose cones in the front fenders, the 1959 Cadillac Cyclone alerted the driver with both an audible signal and warning light of objects in his path. The pitch of the signal would increase as the car grew closer. An ultra-futuristic feature was a one-piece canopy of clear plastic coated with vaporized silver to deflect the sun's rays. It fit snugly against the panoramic windshield to give the driver true 360 degree vision. The canopy was hinged at the rear and was power-operated. It lifted to afford easy entrance for the passenger when either door was opened and disappeared automatically beneath the rear deck for storage when not in use. A very unusual sliding action resulted when the door was opened. At a touch of a button on either side, the door moved outward from the car three inches. The person entering the car then slid the door back along the car for easy entrance. The muffler and exhaust system were located in the front engine compartment with the exhaust outlets just ahead of the front wheels. A communication system allowed occupants of the car to converse with persons outside without retracting the canopy. Only 44 inches high at the top of the laminated plastic canopy, the sleek steel body had an overall length of 196.9 inches. The wheelbase was 104 inches.

1959
De Soto Cella

Instead of using a conventional engine, the Cella was powered by a revolutionary electrochemical system. This power source would transform hydrogen and oxygen into silent electrical energy to drive four lightweight high-speed motors located at the wheels. This conversion to electrical energy would be similar in principal to the operation of a commercial dry-charge battery, wherein electrical energy is generated only when the battery is filled with fluid. With this system, there would be no motor noise. Who copied who with exterior styling is not known, but the Cella had vertical fins on the rear fenders, which the production 1959 Cadillac had in the same year. The De Soto company said the fins were used "as stabilizers to give outstanding directional stability." The Cella had a canopy-type roof which lifted for maximum entrance room. There was a periscopic rear-view mirror on the top of the back roof, and the rear window itself was eliminated, thus providing for better body structure. Heating elements were designed into all glass areas, as well as the periscopic mirror, to eliminate frosting and fogging. The backs of the rear seats were butted against the front seats and faced rearward, and luggage could be placed between the front and rear seats. There was even a refrigeration compartment in the rear wall and a television in the area where the back seat is normally located.

While this roadster could accommodate two persons, it was basically a one-man vehicle. Neither the hood nor the trunk was symmetrical in the traditional design of cars. There was an off-center vertical fin on the trunk similar to an aircraft stabilizer in line with the driver, with a "hump" or long air scoop continuing in front on the left of the hood. There was a curved windshield in front of the driver, and a small auxiliary one for the passenger which folded flat down and was covered when not in use. The passenger seat was lower than the driver's so the wind would not blow on him. The front bumper of the XNR was actually the frame for the grille and was made of heavy stock and so mounted that it absorbed all the shock which normal bumpers could withstand. Similarly, the rear bumper was in the shape of an "X", with the vertical strip extending upward to the tip of the stabilizer and the horizontal piece beneath the luggage compartment. Both front and rear fenders had a slight up and outward flare The high rear fin gave the roadster the overall appearance of a racing car. Unlike in present cars, the muffler and tail pipe ran along the left side of the body beneath the door, from front to rear fender. The entire interior was done up in black leather and aluminum. There was a leather glove box beneath the instrument panel on the passenger's side which could be removed and used as a carrying case with shoulder strap for camera and binoculars.

1 9 6 1
Dodge FliteWing

An innovation of the FliteWing was the use of two "flip" windows in place of the conventional roll-down side windows. This feature facilitated entry and exit and contributed to visibility. The power-operated version of each window automatically rose to a position over the roof when the door handle was moved, remained open until the door was closed, and then descended automatically. A switch in the form of a rubber tape along the lower window sill reversed the electrical circuit when touched, so that arms or fingers could not get pinched by the moving window. The more usual window opening and closing functions were controlled by push buttons. There were several outstanding features of the new window arrangement which made it especially interesting. First, since the windows blended into the roof contour, entrance room was improved. Second, visibility was improved by eliminating the center post between the side windows. Finally, the mechanism to operate the windows was contained in the roof of the car, and was cable-driven by electric motors located in the trunk. The outstanding feature of the new instrument cluster was its emphasis upon providing information to the driver. It contained modern-looking, highly functional instruments that were easy to read. Almost all of the push buttons, switches, and knobs usually located on the instrument panel were placed elsewhere. In the center, the new and unusual speedometer utilized a series of thirteen elliptical "windows" to display car speed in ten-mile-per-hour increments. The left side of the cluster included four rectangular engine instruments (fuel, engine temperature, amperage, and oil pressure) and a parking brake warning light; turn signal and high-beam lights were grouped on the right. Transmission push buttons were located to the left of the cast-aluminum steering wheel on the leading edge of the panel, while the ignition switch was placed in a recess to the right. Other controls (e.g., turn signal lever, light switch, power antenna switch, etc.) were conveniently located on the driver's door panel just ahead of the door handle.

1 9 6 1
Chrysler Turboflite

This car was powered by Chrysler's radical regenerative turbine engine, which weighed half as much as a conventional internal combustion V-8 engine. It had a glass canopy–including windshield–which automatically raised when either door was opened. Side windows were hinged at the roof. Instead of dropping into the doors, the side windows pivoted outward at the bottom, while the windshield wrapped around to the middle of the door on each side. To enter, the passenger first touched the recessed door handle. As the door opened, the canopied roof raised automatically. The door opening was large and unobstructed, making the entrance or exit safe and comfortable. As the door closed, the canopy descended. Immediately below the canopy four red flasher discs were installed to alert the passengers and driver that the roof was returning to its lowered position. The rear of the Turboflite was dominated by a deceleration air-flap suspended between the two stability struts. Adapted from aircraft and racing practice, this air-flap pivoted upwards into the airstream when the hydraulic brakes were applied, creating an air drag to reduce the load on the normal braking system. It was intended for turnpike cruising and could be switched off for lower speeds or city driving.

1961
Ford Gyron

Resembling a sleek racing power boat, this car stood on only two wheels. Ford designers believed that this delta-shaped vehicle, together with the two-wheel concept, might lend itself to the use of a gyroscope for stabilization. This would enable the car to be banked into turns. There was no steering wheel. Steering was done through a dial with separate rings for automatic speed and steering control. The dial, combined with individual accelerator and brake pads on each foot bar, permitted steering from either seat. Two small outrigger wheels toward the rear and on each side of the car were retractable. They could be lowered automatically to balance the vehicle when the gyro was inactive or until it had gained enough momentum to provide stability. The car had an array of computers twenty-five years ahead of its time. As the late George W. Walker, Ford's vice president of styling, noted, "Despite the fact that tremendous changes and improvements in car styling and design have taken place during this century, one aspect of the automobile has been largely unchanged: It has remained basically a rectangular object with a wheel at each corner. In offering the prospect of adequate stability without being restricted to this four-wheel approach, the Gyron exposes countless possibilities to the imagination of the industry."

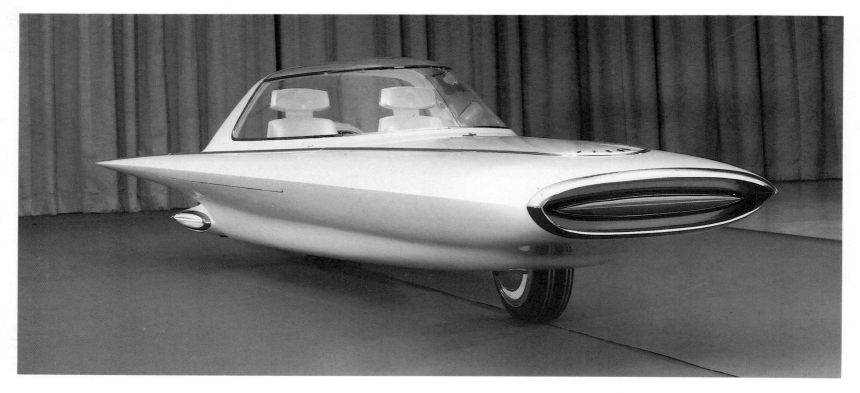

1961-62
Chrysler Turbine

America's most heralded automobile of the early Sixties was a car without a name, a known market, or a predictable price tag. But it had a power plant that conceivably could have challenged the 65-year reign of the internal combustion piston engine. It was called, simply, the Chrysler Corporation Turbine Car. There never had been an automobile introduction quite like that of the Chrysler Turbine Car. Fifty were produced, a large number for an experimental passenger vehicle. The Chrysler-designed bodies were handmade in Italy and shipped to Detroit for final assembly. In October, 1963, a nationwide test program, covering 48 states and Washington, D.C., began with turbine cars assigned to housewives, schoolteachers, students, and salesmen to get reaction. When the mammoth trial run ended on January 28, 1966, the turbines had been driven by 203 people who logged more than a million miles. The car weighed about 200 pounds less than an average piston engine and had 80 percent fewer rotating parts. Virtually a sealed engine, the turbine required no timing, no tuneups, no oil change—and only a single spark plug to ignite it. It could run on unleaded gas, kerosene, or diesel fuel. While the 1963-66 test program got international attention—and fizzled out shortly afterward—Chrysler continued turbine work until 1981, then dropped the project.

93

1 9 6 2
Chevrolet CERV

Obviously the CERV was not intended as a family car. This racing car was built strictly as a research vehicle to test engine, suspension, chassis and braking engineering developments which might be adopted to passenger cars. The name CERV stood for Chevrolet Engineering Research Vehicle. The CERV was a single seater with the engine in the rear and the wheels exposed. The body was made of fiberglass and weighed only 80 pounds. Suspension was independent at all four wheels, and the power transmission was completed through individual axle shafts, each fitted with two universal joints. The rear brakes were inboard to reduce unsprung weight, and the driver had two brake pedals to facilitate braking with either foot. The CERV was powered by a Chevrolet 283-cubic inch V-8 engine that developed 350 horsepower and weighed only 350 pounds. Such specific output, only one pound per horsepower, was rarely achieved in a reciprocating engine. The CERV was timed in speed tests at 172 mph.

1963
Chevrolet Mako Shark I

The basic lines of the Shark were modeled after those of the famous Sting Ray experimental car, forerunner of Corvette Sting Ray. Main elements of this design were the high, pronounced peak line that encircled the body above the wheel openings, and the flat, diving upper body surface with sharply peaked blisters above the wheels and engine. The Shark had four exposed exhaust pipes emerging from a vent in the side of each front fender, pipes which recall in spirit the supercharged sports-classic models of the Thirties. An exposed muffler nestled in a chromed cove in each rocker panel. The twin-bubble top of the Shark was the same design as developed for the XP-700 Chevrolet Corvette experimental car. At its forward edge a raised housing contained a prism-type rear-vision periscope. The plastic roof surface was both tinted and treated inside with vaporized aluminum to deflect sunlight. Shark door handles were flush type, with opening handles that flipped out when an integral button was pressed. In the Shark's rear deck, flush with the trunk lid, were a pair of pop-up safety lights that warned following drivers if the Shark intended to decelerate sharply. Specifically, the lights themselves were recessed in the deck, while a swing-up mirror reflected their beams rearward. The Shark was finished in a varicolored paint scheme based on an iridescent blue upper surface that blended into a white side and underbody, like the natural coloring of a real shark. Normally, no headlights were visible. When the lights were switched on, sections of the grille were electrically rotated on two side pivots to bring the headlights into position.

1 9 6 5
Mako Shark II

Although this model was built on a Chevrolet Corvette chassis and didn't differ much from present Vette styling, it had some interesting innovations. For one, the headrests were suspended over each seat from the ceiling and could be adjusted for height as they dropped down. The steering wheel could be both tilted and telescoped. All control buttons and switches were either recessed or flush with interior surfaces. The forward section of the roof was hinged and lifted easily for entry or exit. It was electrically-powered, controlled by switches in both inner door panels. Located on top of the hood were two round ports through which the driver could check engine oil and water levels. The covers for these were held down by magnetic catches. The entire hood and front fender section swung up and forward for engine service accessibility. The seats did not move at all. They were rigidly secured to the understructure of the car. Instead, there was a "toe-board" and floor controls in front of the driver which were adjustable for accelerator, brake, and dimmer switch. The Shark was equipped with an advanced six-unit headlight system, protected by electrically operated covers when not in use. The right- and left-hand units each contained three lamps in a one-piece reflector. If a light burned out, it showed on the console.

1 9 6 5
Plymouth V.I.P.

V.I.P., of course, means "very important person." And that's who this experimental car ostensibly was designed for. It provided the ultimate in comfort, convenience, communication, entertainment, and freeway travel safety. It contained many items never before built into a passenger car at the time, including an iridescent body paint that changed in various shades from pink to brown, according to the way the light struck it. The driver had a rear-vision scope on the instrument panel (actually a TV screen) which provided a constant picture of the road behind There was a television for the front passenger mounted in the dash, but a 45-degree "divider" on the center console prevented the driver from seeing it. The console ran all the way from the dash to the back seat and contained a tape recorder for dictating letters, a telephone, and controls for a stereophonic system. There was a two-piece all-glass roof. A longitudinal roll bar ran from the windshield to the trunk area, and this acted as a guide to retract either flexible piece of glass into the trunk area. The top was made of a new photochemical glass which darkened upon exposure to light and then cleared again when the light faded. Rear seats reclined into built-in headrests and were so located that passengers, too, could easily watch the television up front.

1966
Corvair Monza

Among the idea cars conceived by Chevrolet in 1966 were two which could have been mistaken for a Corvette, but they were brought out under the "Corvair" name. These were the Monza GT and Monza SS. The Monza GT had a twin canopy. With the touch of a lever, the upper front part swung forward for wide-open access to the passenger compartment, like a clam shell. For servicing, the entire rear body pivoted up to expose all major components of the rear-mounted power plant and drive system. Instead of a rear window, it had open louvers, which could be adjusted–like a Venetian blind–by a lever on the control console. The car had a jet aircraft-type interior, and the driver could actually remove the steering wheel off its column to facilitate entry and exit. Clutch, brake, and accelerator pedals were adjustable. One unique feature on the Monza GT: the horn button was placed on the console between the seats. Slightly shorter than the Monza GT, the Monza SS roadster had conventional doors on either side. It had a standard Corvair engine, placed behind the rear wheels, four carburetors, and a special exhaust system with side outlets. Access to the Monza SS engine was through a conventional deck lid in the rear, similar to the production type Corvair at the time.

1967
Astro I

Astro I had no doors. Instead, an electric swing-back roof and rear section combined with power elevator seats to allow passengers to step upright into the car and sit at armchair height. At a touch of a switch, occupants were lowered to a semi-reclining position beneath a roof that closed down to a height of only 35.5 inches. Three headlamp units on either side of the nose were concealed beneath panels which lowered to expose them. Mounted on the roof was a periscope rear-view mirror that gave passengers a wide-angle rear view over the back of the car. In place of a steering wheel was a twin-grip steering control, adjustable in and out for the driver's comfort. Astro I had an air-cooled single overhead camshaft six-cylinder engine. There was a sliding transmission selector replacing the usual lever. The rear section raised aft of the passenger compartment to allow access to the engine and suspension. A power-actuated canopy moved forward and upward from the passenger compartment to give easy entrance and exit to the specially contoured individual seats. The twin front wheels were steered by power-assisted pistol-grip lever controls. Rear vision was provided by closed circuit television with a viewing screen mounted on a console between the seats. Astro I was built on an 88-inch wheelbase—10 inches shorter than Chevrolet's smallest production coupe, the Corvette. It was slightly shorter and wider than a Corvette, but almost 30 percent lower.

1 9 6 7
Astro II

The air-cooled single overhead camshaft six-cylinder engine used in Astro I was replaced by a liquid-cooled V-8 engine in Astro II. Astro II carried its radiator at the rear, a location intended to minimize the amount of plumbing required and to keep the hot water lines from passing through the passenger compartment. This arrangement freed the front compartment for the storage of luggage. The sponson area on either side of the car behind the passenger compartment was available for extra storage on the left and a collapsible spare tire on the right. Inside, driver and passenger were snug, surrounded by well-padded surfaces which provided a maximum of lateral support–advantageous because of the high maneuverability of this vehicle. A sliding transmission selector replaced the usual lever. The rear section of the Astro II raised immediately aft of the passenger compartment to allow access to the sponson storage areas and to the engine and suspension. The Astro II had a wheelbase of 100 inches, overall length of 181 inches, and a height of a mere 43.7 inches. Overall width was 74 inches.

1967
Ford Seattle-ite XXI

The 1967 Ford Seattle-ite XXI had six wheels–two in back and four steerable ones in front. It had no steering wheel as such. Instead, there was a fingertip-controlled steering dial mounted on a console between driver and passenger. On the dash was a computerized viewing screen which would show information such as estimated arrival time, road conditions, weather, etc. The screen had a rolling map on it which showed the position of the vehicle in relation to the map. Ford designers believed that the tandem mounted wheels would greatly enhance tracking, traction, and braking efficiency. This treatment could make possible a contained, easily interchangeable power capsule. in turn allowing countless design treatments for the trailing vehicle that would house the passenger compartment. Thus a driver could use an economical power capsule of, say, 60 h.p. for short-trip driving, and he could quickly convert to a 400-plus h.p. unit for high speed transcontinental driving. The separate engine compartment could accommodate either hghly sophisticated fuel cells operating electric motors or compact nuclear propulsion devices.

Dodge Charger III

The squatty-looking Dodge Charger III stood only 42 inches high, about five inches shorter than a 1989 Chevrolet Corvette—and resembled the Vette to some degree. Its extremely low structure required a canopy roof which had to lift up about 45 degrees to permit entry. There was a free-standing instrument cluster pod and steering wheel which would swing out of the way as the roof went up. As the pod and steering wheel swung out of the way, the seats automatically pivoted to the desired position for seating. The contoured bucket seats looked much like acceleration bucket seats from a space capsule. A recessed handle in the pod permitted the driver to pull the steering wheel down in front of him and lock. There was no need to raise the hood to check service items such as water, oil, or battery levels, but, instead, a small "service hatch" on the lower fender on the driver's side. There was no rear window. A periscope-type rearview mirror raised up out of a special door in the roof. The mirror provided wide-angle coverage to the rear. Synchronized with the regular braking system was a spoilertype three-flap braking unit at the rear end. These provided additional braking, as in present jet planes. When the flaps of the spoiler brakes went up, stop lights concealed underneath flashed to give warning that the Charger was slowing down.

1 9 6 9
Buick Century Cruiser

Designed originally as the Firebird IV in 1964-65, this experimental car became the 1969 Buick Century Cruiser. It was a high-performance car designed for cross-country cruising on automatic highways of the future. While traveling the automatic highway, Century Cruiser would provide the comforts of a living room on wheels for four passengers, with semi-reclining, swiveling contour seats, television, a pull-out table, and a built-in refrigerator. An entrance canopy, including the entire glass area and most of the roof, would slide forward and upward, and a door on each side would pull out and glide forward to provide easy stand-up entrance and exit. The canopy and doors would open automatically at the touch of a button. For extra stability under high wind conditions, blades extended forward on both sides past the front wheel, and two rear blades raised above the sloping deck surface to a height of about ten inches. Front side panels fit close to the wheels, and a section of each would move outward to allow wheel clearance as the car turned. In manual operation, the driver used hand grips in the armrests. When on an automatic highway, he would put a punch card programmed for his route into a slot and transfer control to the electronic system. Century Cruiser had a luggage compartment at the front which would raise for easy access height.

1 9 6 9
Ford Techna

This model featured revolutionary power-operated parallel-hinged doors. By opening straight out from the body, rather than swinging out, the two six-foot-wide doors provided the same easy entry as with four doors, even when the car was parked within 18 inches of another vehicle. The car provided sweeping vision with a glass windshield which eliminated the front corner posts. The entire front end–hood and fenders–was one piece, and it pivoted forward for complete access to the engine compartment and front suspension. There was a unique "inspection hatch" in the center of the hood.

You simply lifted it up to check oil, coolant, transmission fluid, power steering, carburetor, and distributor, instead of lifting the entire hood. The car had twin aluminum radiators mounted at a 50-degree angle relative to the ground. Alternator and air-conditioning units were placed at the rear rather than front of the engine, and the battery was placed in the trunk. In addition to conventional rear lights mounted within the rear bumper, supplemental brake and turn signal lamps were located in the rear window. These high level lamps could be seen through successively following cars in heavy traffic.

1969
Plymouth Duster I

This model was a high performance concept of Chrysler Corp.'s popular Road Runner muscle car in the late 1960s. It featured the usual low curved racing type of windshield and had airplane-type flaps (called spoilers) on the top and sides. There was a set of adjustable spoilers on the side of the rear fender near the gas tank filler cap to prevent side-to-side yaw when slipstreaming in a race, and even two of them on top behind the driver, plus spoilers in the front rock shields to reduce frontal lift. The car carried a 426 hemi engine, one of Chrysler's powerful power plants at the time.

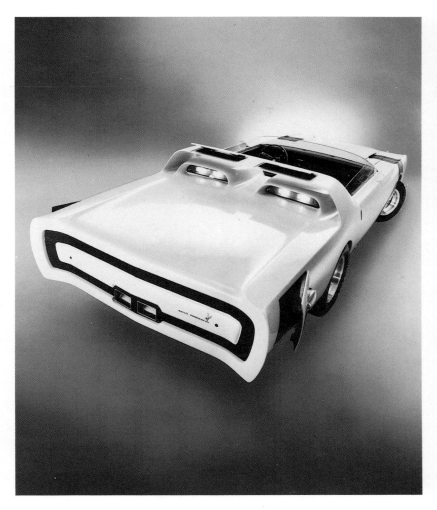

1 9 6 9
Chrysler Concept 70X

This model had doors that worked on parallelogram hinges, allowing passengers to get in and out of the rear seat without folding down the front seat. The driver's side front door opened out and slid forward parallel to the body, while the rear door opened out and rearward. On the passenger side of the car there was only one huge door which slid to the rear, as on present-day vans. The door locks functioned much like the locking rods of a bank vault door. By turning a handle in the door trim panel, the occupant would send a rod horizontally from the vertical shut face of the doors into a pocket in the pillar. This would provide an interlock which would resist door intrusion during side impact and door opening during rear impact. Windshield pillars were very slender.

An electric device on the rear-view mirror made the driver much more aware of traffic conditions around him. Imbedded in the bottom of the mirror were three small red lights—a proximity warning device. With this device, a small ultrasonic unit was mounted next to the rear seat speaker and swept an area 50 feet to the rear in three zones—the left lane, and lane immediately behind the car, and the right lane. Vehicles in any of the zones would light the respective light on the mirror, automatically indicating when traffic entered or left any of the three lanes.

1970
Ford Estate

One of the most talked about new-idea cars at 1970 auto shows was a car which recalled the "Golden Age of Motorcars." The Ford Estate Coupe was designed to look like a rich man's car. The rear was reminiscent of many of yesteryear's cars with its "bustle back" design, a design which makes the trunk a prominent feature. From its appearance here, however, it looks as if the trunk had space enough for only a set of golf clubs, judging by the small trunk lid. Just as reminiscent of the past was the "landaulet" half roof which covered the rear seat passenger compartment. There was actually no cover made for the front passengers—strictly open-air it was. The Estate combined interior luxury with sport-car flair. The Estate actually was a production Ford Maverick model reconstructed for auto shows, and never to appear again.

1973
Chevrolet XP 898

Built with a frameless fiberglass foam sandwich body and chassis, this two-place sports coupe offered a unique look at alternative engineering approaches to future techniques in design and manufacturing. The entire body consisted of four lightweight fiberglass outer body panels—the floor pan, firewall, upper front, and upper rear—with a rigid urethane foam filling the designed clearance between the panels. The structure and appearance of the car were designed so that the body could be assembled using four lightweight molded outer skin sections. With the outer skin panels placed in a foaming mold, liquid urethane was injected between the panels where it expanded and bonded the body into a single, rigid sandwich structure. The result was a vehicle body virtually free of squeaks, rattles, and vibrations. Once the urethane hardened (which took about fifteen minutes), the suspension drive train, hood, and doors were bolted to reinforcing plates which were bonded to the fiberglass panels. Of conventional front engine, rear drive, the XP 898 used many components from the Chevrolet Vega. The vehicle had a 90-inch wheelbase with an overall length of 166 inches. A key consideration in the engineering design of the XP 898 was the advantage of improved crash-worthiness of the sandwich construction technique. The energy absorption characteristics of the vehicle enabled engineers to simulate crash conditions for the vehicle at speeds up to 50 miles per hour without catastrophic failure to the structure.

1 9 7 6
Ford Prima

This concept was a predecessor to an almost identical car Ford designed in 1979, the Fiesta Fantasy. Both models were four vehicles in one. The Prima was basically a small two-seat pickup truck. With special removable clip-on panels, it could be converted to a fastback model, station wagon, or two-seat coupe. (See 1979 Ford Fiesta Fantasy, pages 128-129.)

1 9 7 7 - 7 8
Ford Megastar I and II

Riding in the Megastar made one feel as if he were flying in an executive jet plane with its enormous side windows. Eighty percent of the car's front doors was glass, and the panoramic windshield curved up into the roof over the driver's and passenger's heads. There were two versions built–a four-door Megastar I in 1977 and a two-door Megastar II in 1978. Notice the changes made from one model to the other. The original Megastar had a sharply raised rear roof with a squared off hump in back for more room. The hump was rounded off on Megastar II to give it a more "hatchback" look.

1 9 7 8
Mercury XM

While most of the concept cars produced by Detroit during the past fifty years had a touch of the Space Age, this one went backward in time. It re-introduced the rumble seat, an open-air design of the 1930s. The car was basically a two-seater. But by simply raising the rear hatch window and flipping back the decklid, a rumble seat emerged and the car was transformed into a four-passenger model, with the rear passengers getting the exterior breeze.

1 9 7 8
Chevrolet Astro-Vette

An experimental Chevrolet Corvette, this model had a low slanted windshield to minimize aerodynamic drag. It had a very long sloping hood and a smooth-flowing rear deck without any protrusions which would stop air flow over the surfaces. Air intakes on both sides of the front fenders helped cool the engine. These were louvered and would open when actuated by pressure. The underside of the entire body had partial belly-pans to reduce the air disturbances which normally occur between the underside of a car and the road. There was a roll bar behind the driver which was given an inverted air foil shape to further minimize drag. There were flush aluminum wheel discs and skirts over the rear wheel openings.

1978
Pontiac Trans AM Type K

This station wagon had the tailgates hinged on either side of the body, instead of in the rear. The rear window—unlike present station wagons—was fixed and mounted vertically above three black glass slots running the full width. When the brakes were applied, or lights turned on, the black stripe would glow red, accomplished by mounting conventional red taillights behind the black-tinted Plexiglas. While the rear window did not open, there was full access to the interior from either side. The side windows were released by a console-mounted pull-lever and cable arrangement, with the levers recessed inside the doorjambs so they could not be accidentally unlatched. There was excellent vision to the rear with mirrors right, left, and center. When all the rear seats were folded down, looking back from the driver's seat gave one the impression that he was in a long all-glass tube. When closed, the gull-wing windows rested against thick soft-rubber gaskets, making tight seals against wind and rain.

1 9 7 9
Ford Probe I

Designed as the "typical car of the 1980s," Probe I was said to have the ideal aerodynamic shape. The sleek-surfaced car achieved an "air drag" rating of .22 in extensive wind-tunnel tests, lower than any American car on the market at the time. (Drag measures a car's wind resistance.) With such sleekness, Ford claimed the Probe could achieve a fuel economy of 39 miles per gallon in city driving. Probe's interior suggested a modern living-room atmosphere to eliminate boredom on long freeway-type drives. It had an electronic entertainment center, allowing riders to play games or watch television,

and the ultimate in stereo sound. Headrests were electrically controlled, and the car could be started with a universal credit card instead of keys. The car was made of composite body panels, including extensive use of plastic alloys and thin glass. The aerodynamic effect was carried out further with the use of clear plastic wheel covers and plastic fender skirts, which were hinged and tilted out for removing a wheel. The Probe was about the size of a Ford Mustang of the time, measuring 188.5 inches long.

1979
Ford Fiesta Fantasy

One could convert the Ford Fiesta Fantasy into four different vehicles by simply switching easy-to-install modules on the rear section–from a two-seat pickup truck into a two-seat sports coupe, 2 plus 2 soft-top convertible, or a four-passenger station wagon. Its design features made it a viable approach for meeting the demand for an economical, versatile, and fuel-efficient small car. It offered a soft tonneau cover on the pickup version. Lightweight fiberglass tops clamped easily onto both sides of the pickup's cargo box to form the Fantasy's four other models. A removable glass-and-aluminum bulkhead separated the passenger compartment from the rear section of the pickup and sports coupe versions of the vehicle. When folded down, the rear seat formed a portion of the cargo bed on the pickup and provided for additional cargo area in the station wagon, convertible and 2 plus 2 hardtop models. It also served as a rumble seat on the pickup truck when the bulkhead dividing the passenger compartment from the pickup bed was removed. The powertrain and wheelbase were similar to Ford's German-built Fiesta. Built on a 90-inch wheelbase, it had a four-cylinder transverse-mounted engine and front-wheel drive. Interior features included tan contoured leather front-bucket seats and a rear seat that folded down to form part of the cargo floor on the pickup version in addition to permitting additional carrying capacity for the fastback and station wagon models.

1 9 8 0
Ford Probe II

Although its exterior design was not spectacular, Ford's Probe II cannot be overlooked. Between 1979 and 1985 Ford created five concept models named the Probe— Probe I, II, III, IV and V. In 1988 Ford actually produced a car called Probe, and it went on sale to the public, but it bore no resemblance to any previous Probes. Ford Probe II was a plain-Jane looking car, resembling almost any other sterotyped car on the road today. The concept Probe II was described in press releases as a "compact and fuel-efficient car which could be in production for 1985." It never did reach the assembly line. A diesel engine was planned for Probe II, but that, too, never got off the drawing board. (See other Ford Probes in this book.)

1980
Mercury Antser

One of the biggest features of this car was a huge electronic map display which took up the entire dashboard on the passenger side. It could be programmed to give detours and alternate routes around accidents and other traffic problems. As a safety measure, the Antser's highly sophisticated electronic instrument panel continuously displayed the computer-calculated average distance required to stop the car under current operating conditions. The doors would move outward a few inches and slide back for entrance. Seats could be inflated with air pressure to suit the driver and passenger comfort.

1 9 8 1
Ford Shuttler

A tiny-tiny midget was the Ford Shuttler. Its overall length was 129 inches, nearly two feet shorter than the smallest new American entry into the U.S. market in 1989, the Chevrolet Geo Metro (146 inches). It was even smaller than the smallest car sold in the U.S. at present, the imported Yugo, which stretches 139 inches bumper to bumper. The Shuttler was a mere 50 inches high and 61 inches wide. Of course it fitted only two small people. Or, as one Chevrolet public relations staffer always would quip when asked how many persons a certain model could seat: "Four fat people, or eight small children."

1 9 8 1
Ford Pockar

Some conventional cars, especially luxury models, have big pockets on the inside of doors for storing magazines and other documents. This car had them on the outside—for storage of luggage. Both side doors were cut horizontally at midpoint, and the bottom part dropped down like the tailgate of a pickup truck. As the name suggests, the Pockar was a "pocket car" for commuting in and out of town. In addition to the two lockable compartments in the doors, there was ample additional space inside for luggage and four passengers. When used for only two people, the Pockar had a rear seat that could be folded down flat, a design feature found on many of today's cars. Earlier designs for such urban vehicles rarely included space for luggage and four passengers. The side door luggage compartments protruded into the interiors of the doors and served as armrests. There were electronic displays on the dashboard in a semi-circular fashion (or half moon) which could be seen easily through the upper half of the steering wheel. Huge side-view mirrors were integrated with the side body and hood design as a single horizontal streamlined unit.

Unlike present cars which are not protected underneath from road dirt and sludge, Probe III had a unique under-body pan, which ran from front to rear and helped smoothen the air flow under the car. The pan incorporated an automatically adjustable front section which was controlled electrically and lowered at speeds above 25 mph to form a special ground effect to reduce drag and lift at speed. Below 25 mph, where the aerodynamic effect is less critical and in towns where the front section in the lowered position could be damaged when the car was parked close to high curbs, it was automatically retracted into the raised position. Instead of the usual single piece, there were twin rear spoilers, one on top of the other, to smoothen the air flow over the back of the car. Wheel covers were flat with tiny holes around their circumference to admit air for cooling the brakes. Rear aerodynamics also were improved by a lip located under the rear bumper which ensured that the air left the car in a controlled manner and reduced dirt collection on the rear lamp. The conventional drip rail mouldings, usually placed on the roof over the doors, were eliminated, and the drain channels were designed behind the tops of the doors and flush fitting glass. To control turbulence around the wheels, narrow section low-profile tires were mounted on narrow rims. The "rocker panels," the piece of body metal that curves underneath the doors, were bent inward in the middle of the car for aesthetics and easier entry and exit.

1981
GM Aero X

Probably one of the most notable design features of this car was the absence of exterior mouldings and flush glass all around. This study in aerodynamics represented the latest example of a fuel-efficient car, designed without sacrificing aesthetics or comfort. The hood sloped down in a gentle curve and used a unique "under the nose" cooling air inlet. The wheel covers were flush with the wheels, and wheels were mounted in line with the body sides to give the car a total "slippery" configuration. The rear of the body was shaped so that air flowed smoothly over it. The body was fiberglass. The car underbody—from the air inlet rearward to the front axle—was carefully shaped. A pair of progressive widening wedge forms began under the nose and reached their maximum width at the front of each wheel opening. This insured that the air which was not needed for engine cooling was deflected efficiently under the car. Aerodynamic tests have shown that the wheelhouse space usually required for wheel movements in bumps and turns contributes to overall drag. In the Aero X, each wheel opening incorporated a unique flexible spacer which smoothed the airflow along the entire body side and permitted all the necessary wheel motions.

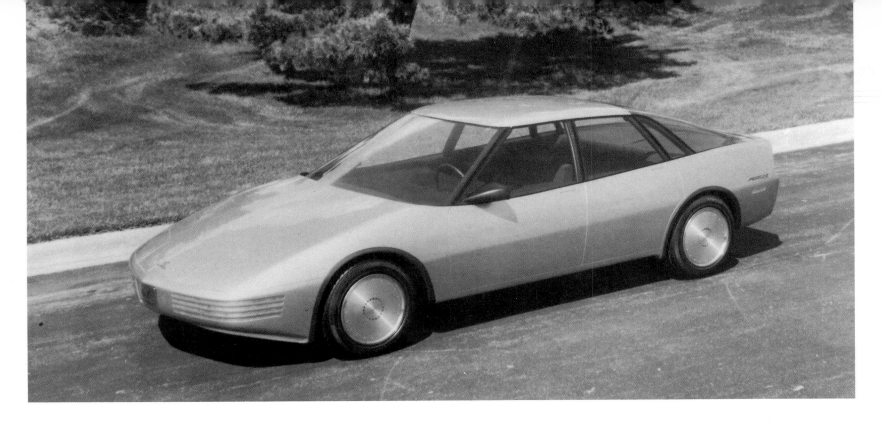

1 9 8 1
Ford Cockpit

Ford claimed that this concept car achieved fuel economy of better than 75 miles per gallon in city driving. The three-wheeled car, which seated two persons in tandem, was so named because it resembled the cockpit of a fighter plane. The hinged canopy lifted up hydraulically forward. The car was powered by a 12-horsepower, 200cc single-cylinder motorcycle-like engine, mounted–of all places–inside the rear wheel. A possible urban commuter car of the future, the Cockpit offered the dual advantage of outstanding fuel economy linked with optimum cruising speed to provide acceptable inter-city highway transportation in a period of a severe energy crisis. The tiny car had a triangular chassis which, with additional side support bars, carried all mechanical components. The transverse-spring front suspension was controlled by hydraulic shock absorbers, while the rear-mounted powerplant and driving wheel were set at the apex of the chassis and sprung by two integral coil spring shock absorber units. The car's windshield was made of laminated glass while the whole canopy and rear window were of tinted reinforced plastic.

1 9 8 2
GM Lean Machine

General Motors Corp. described this one as "what may be the first new road vehicle invented during this century." The Lean Machine—named for its slender silhouette and tilting capabilities—was similar to a motorcycle in size and weight, could accelerate to 60 mph in seven seconds, and travel up to 200 miles on a gallon of gas. However, significant differences that separate the two vehicles may give the Lean Machine an edge over the motorcycle in futuristic transportation systems. The vehicles part company principally in their suspension systems, aerodynamics, and passenger accommodations—or lack thereof. The motorcycle is an inherently unstable vehicle that must be propped upon its two wheels when it is not moving, and its rider is totally exposed. Not so the Lean Machine. It had one wheel in front, but two more in back gave it an independent three-point stand. Furthermore, the rider was enclosed in a fiberglass and clear plastic shell. This elongated passenger pod, pivoting at either end above the power pod, rotates horizontally and separately from the lower unit. Pedals control the rotation, enabling the rider to lean into a turn as cyclists do to lower and move inward the center of gravity, the tricycle power unit remaining upright. The passenger compartment had all of the amenities of an automobile, including protection during inclement weather. Steering, braking, and throttle controls were combined in handlebars while an automatic transmission linked to a rear-mounted, liquid-cooled, 30-horsepower engine, shifted gears.

1 9 8 2
Ford Flair

While there was nothing that unusual about this car's exterior styling, it was an experiment in the use of two-piece fiberglass reinforced polyester material for all body panels. The open-top car also demonstrated the use of a new type of phone system. Unlike the typical mobile-telephone installation with hand-held receiver, the car itself was a telephone. With its integrated "hands-free" phone system, calls could be placed by using a 12-button keyboard of the vehicle's computer-controlled "message center." The caller spoke into a microphone built into the driver's sun visor. The other party was heard through the rear speakers of the car's entertainment system. The windshield and side and back windows were made of bronze-tinted glass. The back window was hinged and could be opened electrically in the same fashion as conventional power windows on today's cars.

1982
GM Aero 2000

There was no conventional circular steering wheel in this car, nor brake pedals or accelerator. Instead, the driver used an aircraft-type vertical "stick" mounted on the center console, which controlled steering, braking, and throttling. Also, the driver did not have to take his eyes from the road to see car speed, fuel supply, and similar readings. They were reflected in the windshield–known today as a "heads-up" display. Like switching a channel on a television set, road maps could be called up on a screen on the dashboard. In place of a rear-view mirror there was a video camera which provided a 180-degree view of the rear. There were even radar-assisted brakes. A single sliding door on each side moved far enough back to provide as much access to the rear seat as a traditional two-door car. The power windows and air conditioning/heating system could be activated by spoken commands using electronics that were able to recognize and respond to voices for which they were programmed. The suspension system could be adjusted up or down for city or high-speed driving. The car had moveable front-wheel skirts and a spoiler which could be extended from the lower rear body to improve the aerodynamic shape. There was a unique experimental design for lap-shoulder belts. The reels which take up the belts were built into the seats themselves, and the belts only needed to be slipped into a slot in the center console, not buckled as they are today.

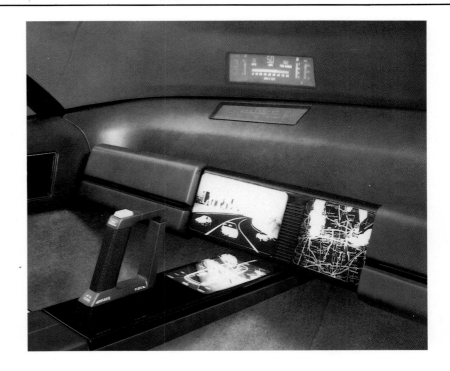

1 9 8 2
GM TPC

TPC meant "Two Person Commuter." It was one of the lightest concept cars ever built. It weighed just 1,070 lbs., compared with 2,200 lbs. for the Chevrolet Chevette, General Motors' lowest weight production car at that time. Contributing to the lightness were the front end, doors, and rear fenders, all of which were aluminum. There were no sharp body lines–everything was "rounded," including side windows, which "ballooned" outward. Even the rear-view mirrors were eliminated from the outside and mounted inside instead. GM claimed the TPC was so aerodynamically slippery that it could squeeze 95 miles from a gallon of gas on the highway, around 68 mpg in typical commuter traffic. The sleek design of the car produced very little airstream turbulence, causing the car to flow with a very low aerodynamic drag coefficient of .31. Other contributing factors to the car's aerodynamic success were flush glass, the rear-view mirrors mounted inside the passenger compartment, tires flush with the wheelhouse and wheels flush with the tires, tapered front fenders, a sloped hood, extended roof ventilation air flow underneath the roof extension, an air dam that was integral with the front end panel, and large radii on front panels and windshield pillars. The TPC was powered by a tiny .8 liter three-cylinder engine coupled with a five-speed manual transmission. It had a four-gallon fuel tank.

1 9 8 3
Ford Probe IV

This super-aerodynamic car had a drag coefficient (Cd) of only .15, which is roughly equivalent to that of a jet fighter. According to Ford, this was the lowest of any conventional five-door vehicle in the world. If a typical car of today had such a low Cd, it would achieve 20 percent better fuel economy at a steady speed of 55 miles per hour. The most striking exterior features included rubber fender skirts which covered nearly the entire wheels (they turned out with the wheels), flush curved glass over the entire top section, and a streamlined hood and nose that dropped to the bumper area. To make possible the very low hood, the engine was included 70 degrees forward. There were no grille apertures for cooling. The radiator and air-contidioning condenser were placed in the rear, with air intakes and an electric fan behind the rear-wheel wells. The car had an automatic height adjustment system. At higher speeds the front of the body dropped to four inches ground clearance. It would lift up to 6.5 inches at lower speeds. At the same time, the rear of the car would rise six inches. A front deployable air dam had a manual override for operating on rough roads or for faster driving. A departure from the straight back design, the front seats had a special sling configuration which included lumbar and thigh support that could be adjusted for a variety of individual pressure points.

1983
Continental Concept 100

If you look at a photo of this car, you'll see nothing unusual about its exterior styling. But the Concept 100 had what was believed to be the largest number of functioning advanced electronic features ever built into a single vehicle. And they weren't frivolous gadgets. They all operated. The car even talked to the driver and obeyed his commands. If he said, for example, "Headlamps on,"

the lamps turned on. A sonar detection system warned the driver if there were any obstacles in the car's path—other cars, children or a bike in the drive—both front and rear. A satellite navigation system called Tripmonitor, mounted in the dash, told him at all times his location on a TV screen map and could plot his route as he was driving. There were gauges which told him when tire pressures were low via a blinker on the dash. Other electronic wizardry included a hand-held transmitter for locating the car in a parking lot (the car would blow the horn and flash the lights when the transmitter was aimed at all) and another transmitter which turned the ignition on or off from a distance and opened and locked the doors. Another computer on the dash warned if anything under the hood needed attention. The upper portion of the rear window contained brake lights on both the left and right sides (conventional cars now have only one in the center). Concept 100 even had a TV screen and computers in the rear compartment for children to play games and tapes, using their own earphones.

CONTINENTAL CONCEPT 100

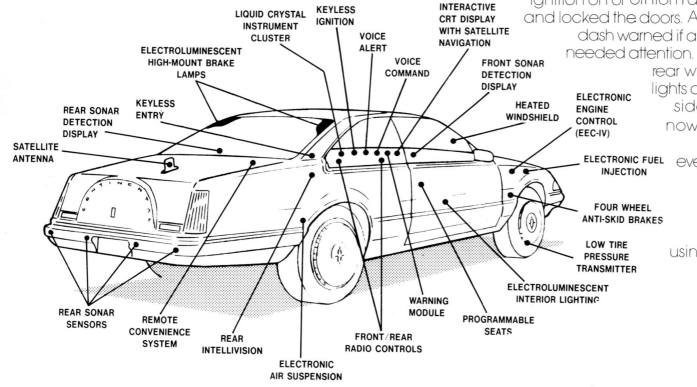

LIQUID CRYSTAL INSTRUMENT CLUSTER

KEYLESS IGNITION

VOICE ALERT

VOICE COMMAND

INTERACTIVE CRT DISPLAY WITH SATELLITE NAVIGATION

ELECTROLUMINESCENT HIGH-MOUNT BRAKE LAMPS

FRONT SONAR DETECTION DISPLAY

KEYLESS ENTRY

HEATED WINDSHIELD

ELECTRONIC ENGINE CONTROL (EEC-IV)

REAR SONAR DETECTION DISPLAY

SATELLITE ANTENNA

ELECTRONIC FUEL INJECTION

FOUR WHEEL ANTI-SKID BRAKES

LOW TIRE PRESSURE TRANSMITTER

ELECTROLUMINESCENT INTERIOR LIGHTING

REAR SONAR SENSORS

REMOTE CONVENIENCE SYSTEM

REAR INTELLIVISION

ELECTRONIC AIR SUSPENSION

FRONT/REAR RADIO CONTROLS

WARNING MODULE

PROGRAMMABLE SEATS

1983
Buick Questor

Even the steering wheel column of the Questor was carpeted, and the instrument panel had no instruments except a TV monitor which provided an unobstructed wide-angle view to the rear. There were no outside rear-view mirrors nor door handles. Most gauges and other controls were placed in the center of the steering wheel and on the console between the seats. A laser key system operated on an invisible light beam. Pressing a switch contained in a hand-held unit about half the size of a garage door opener caused the car to rise about six inches for easier entry. The laser key unlocked and opened the door and turned on all on-board systems–including the pop-up systems sentinel–and automatically adjusted the seat, pedals, steering column, and

entertainment and interior systems to the personal settings of the driver. When the doors were closed, the car automatically lowered to driving position. The laser key was used in place of a traditional ingition key. Pressing it again put Questor in the accessory mode; the system sentinel dropped out of sight and the rear-view TV monitor, navigation center, and touch command center were activated. When the engine was running, an instrument panel rose from the base of the windshield. Since the panel was transparent, it did not interfere with the driver's view of the road. When the car reached 25 mph, the front nosed down for better fuel economy and aerodynamics. The rear rose up three inches when highway speeds were reached.

1 9 8 4
Chevrolet Citation IV

Said to be the most aerodynamic car built by Chevrolet, this car had a drag coefficient of .265, lower than the sleek Corvette. Lowering the drag factor alone allows for substantial increase in fuel economy. The Citation IV had a potential fuel economy in the 60 mpg range. Drag is the resistance of air to the passage of a body through it. In contemporary vehicles aerodynamic drag constitutes about half of the total rolling resistance when moving at 50 miles per hour. Just about all design features of the Citation IV were flush with each other. The windshield sloped down 68 degrees, and the angle continued straight down to the grille. In keeping with the smooth exterior surfaces, the door handles and key locks were eliminated. To open the doors, you simply entered a four-digit combination of numbers on a computer-controlled switch in the vertical pillar at the upper right side of the door. Digital speedometer readings were reflected off the inside of the windshield. Pod-mounted controls were at fingertip distance from the steering wheel. An angled center console bridged the area between the armrest and the deep padded dash. It housed an electric stereo receiver, electric mirror controls, and the shift lever.

1 9 8 5
Ford T2008

You would never have to be worried about being stranded should this car break down. It had a satellite communication system that automatically diagnosed the problem and contacted the nearest Ford dealer to let them know where you were. A prime design feature of the car was its modular design, meaning you could switch different bodies on the same base car any time you desired—from any type of family car to a light truck. This concept also simplified repairs. You simply exchanged modules instead of repairing a certain component. The Ford T2008 was designed to run on automatically guided highways, which would be reserved strictly for such vehicles. Simply press a button on a special map and the car would guide you to your destination automatically, until you told it to change course. Electronic gadgets in the car would do all the maneuvering for you in case of upcoming hazards or "road hog" drivers. Electronically controlled front and rear screens would give the car's exact location and references to nearby highways. Just a few of the other wizardry features of the T2008: an automatic keyless entry system that eliminates door handles and keyholes; an infrared display system that enhances vision at night and in bad weather; cameras which replace rear-view mirrors; four-wheel steering; a glass roof which "captures" the day's heat and stores it until you need warmth.

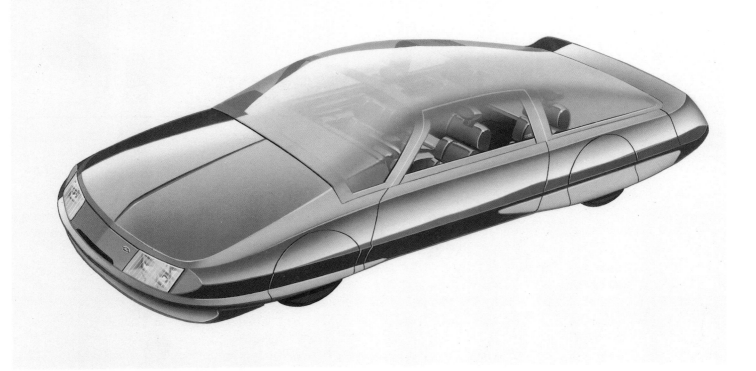

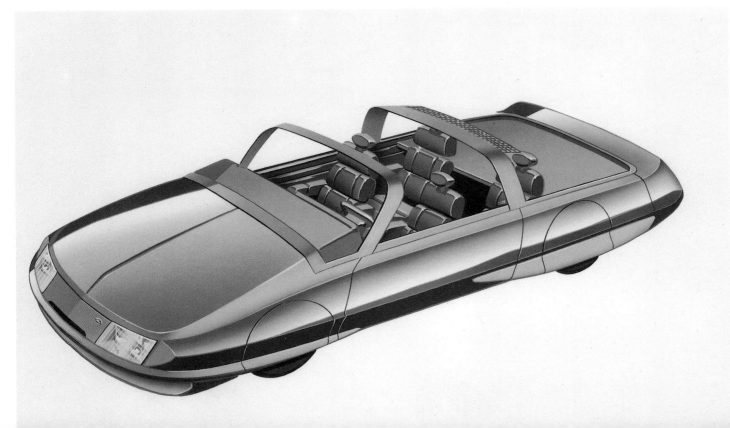

1 9 8 5
Cadillac Cimarron

The vehicle, a convertible built on a Cadillac Cimarron platform, featured two wind-shields, exotic built-in electronics, televisions for both front and rear consoles, and a cellular telephone controlled from a fixed hub steering wheel for "hands off" talking. Cadillac displayed the concept Cimarron alongside a classic 1931 dual cowl tour-ing sedan from which its two-windshield design was inspired. These two unique Cadillacs shared a striking design element, but demonstrated in every other aspect the dramatic advances of more than fifty years of innovative automotive engineer-ing. Individually, the shape and content of each vehicle made a statement about the culture of its era. The 1931 Fleetwood had a 148 inch wheelbase, weighed 6,200 pounds, was powered by a 16-cylinder V-type engine, and contained foot cushions, robe straps, and a clock that required rewinding every eight days. The concept Cimar-ron, on the other hand, had a 106.2 inch wheelbase, weighed 3,380 pounds, was powered by a specially built front transverse-mounted 2.8 liter multi-port fuel-injected V-6 engine and contained televisions, two-way radios with headsets, a telephone, and electronic panels that told passengers in both front and rear compartments the status of various engine functions.

1 9 8 5
Ford Probe V

Ford claimed this fiberglass concept car was "the most aerodynamic driveable car in the world." Probe's coefficient of drag (or Cd) was 0.137, about the same as an F15 jet fighter plane. Probe's features included fully skirted front and rear wheels and all-glass upper body and sliding doors. The glass was actually sculpted into the body -- there was not a separate windshield, sideglass, or rear window. The rear window ran right down into the bumper area. A dorsal fin on top of the rear trunk helped stabilize the car. On the interior there was a swept-away instru-

ment panel with tilt and telescoping instrumentation pod and steering wheel, and a "heads-up" display, which is a speedometer imbedded in the windshield in front of the driver's vision. The engine was mounted midship behind the rear seat. Instead of being raised like a tailgate, the glass hood popped up one inch and slid rearward. The seat cushions operated like a roller blind. When used as a seat, they could be pulled out; if you needed storage for grocery bags, it could be rolled back up.

1 9 8 5
Buick Wildcat

"It's one of the wildest cars we've ever designed," said Charles M. Jordan, GM's director of design, when describing the experimental Wildcat. The mid-engine car had no traditional doors. There was a canopy which raised forward. As it raised, the steering wheel tilted upward for ease of entry. With the canopy raised, the driver or passenger sat on a low, wide sill and swung his or her legs into the compartment. The dashboard was clear of instruments. Most were housed in the stationary hub of the steering wheel, including oil pressure, battery, fuel level, and coolant temperature gauges. Directly in the driver's line of vision was a little see-through panel on the dash which showed speed. Actually, it was the only instrument on the dash in front of the driver. In the center of the dash was a three-dimensial "Spark Map" (resembling a small TV screen), which gave various engine readings. Several other displays revealed such information as "G" forces experienced in a turn, horsepower and torque, spark function for precise engine tuning, percent of tire slippage, low air pressure warnings for all four tires, direction of travel (with electronic compass), and oil temperature.

1986
Ford Vignale TSX-6

This was a multifunction vehicle which could be used as a station wagon, passenger car, or pickup truck. The Vignale had a raised roof which slid forward electrically to convert it quickly into an open-air cargo vehicle. The rear windows could be flipped up for loading or unloading. The Vignale had three rows of seats on a mid-sized platform. There was seating for two in the front row, three in the middle row, and two in the last row. All seats were forward facing. The raised roof enabled the second and third row passengers to sit higher than the front seat passengers, thus providing better visibility and a feeling of spaciousness for passengers in the last two rows. The seat-folding system was designed to serve a dual function: the middle and rear rows of seats could be folded to make a double bed or a completely flat loading platform. A third option was a single bed plus half of the total loading capacity.

1 9 8 6
Pontiac Trans Sport Van

While all car companies were designing scores of experimental cars, no one thought of applying space-age technology to the ordinary van. In 1986 Pontiac became the first U.S. car company to show us a look at what the mini-van of the future might look like. It called the new concept the Trans Sport Mini-Van. The side windows wrapped into the roof, and the windshield extended well back over the driver in a helicopter-like bubble form. The look was adapted in the 1989 Pontiac Transport, Olds Silhouette, and Chevrolet Lumina, but these do not possess the prototype's more futuristic elements. The abundance of glass allowed the vehicle to sport a light emitting diode on the windshield, which projected speed and other driver information–known as a "heads-up" display. The Trans Sport Van had a gull-wing door on the right side, and door handles were recessed. Other features included a personal computer recessed into the passenger side of the instrument panel which incorporated a pop-up screen and keyboard access features such as weather reports, accident reports and detours, navigational directions, calculator functions, and the ability to schedule air travel and make hotel reservations. A windshield-mounted overhead console with a scanning screen replaced the conventional rear-view mirror. A television-like display featuring a digital readout measured the distance of approaching traffic. Middle and rear-seat passengers could even view a small television mounted in an overhead console centered behind the driver and front passenger seats.

1986
Corvette Indy

Unlike many other futuristic cars, this one had at least one unusual feature. Electronic displays on the sides of each door housed radio and climate controls, plus a computer navigational TV screen. On the top center of the dashboard was a camera which provided rear vision. In addition to featuring four-wheel drive, the Corvette Indy had a four-wheel steering system. By a slight adjustment, you could steer it with front wheels alone or all four wheels. Rear-wheel steering enhanced low-speed cornering and maneuverability, and provided improved high-speed handling. For optimum braking, the Corvette Indy was equipped with anti-lock brakes. Magnetic wheel rotation sensors detected impending wheel lock-up under braking and transmitted a signal to the wheel control system computer. If any wheel decelerated at a faster rate than another, brake pressure was reduced to that wheel. Just as in modern fighter aircraft, where mechanical control links and hydraulics have been replaced with electronic actuation, a computer-controlled system on Corvette Indy employed a sensor that read gas pedal position. This information went to a computer, which activated an electric motor to open or close the throttle.

1 9 8 7
Chevrolet Blazer XT-1

Chevrolet called its new 1987 vehicle a "truck," but it really looked like a nifty little van any sportsman would be elated to tool around in on weekends at his favorite getaway place. The four-wheel drive utility vehicle had a body that dropped down for easy entry, shifted automatically into four-wheel drive when needed, had glass all around that made it look like a "greenhouse," and was equipped with thirty computers that checked vehicle operations. Four-wheel long-travel independent suspension allowed each Blazer XT-1 wheel to travel up to 10.5 inches to individually adjust to changes in the road surface, jostling passengers less and preventing loads from shifting. The driver could also set the suspension characteristics and trim heights differently, depending on the terrain. The vehicle could drop up to one inch for easier entry for the driver and passengers, and could be set up to four inches higher for rough, off-road exploring. Four-corner leveling compensated for uneven load distribution. The transfer case included a self-sensing, self-actuating four-wheel-drive operation that automatically shifted the Blazer XT-1 into four-wheel drive when it sensed that a wheel was beginning to slip. A computer maximized performance by sensing slip and shifting torque fore or aft as much as 30 percent to the other axle while the vehicle was running in four-wheel drive.

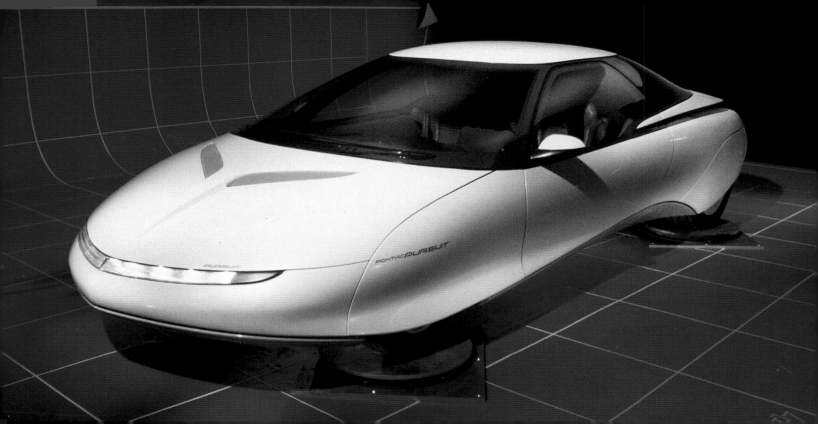

1987
Pontiac Pursuit

Probably the most outstanding innovation on this car–which resembled a space ship from "Star Trek" – was four-wheel steering, a new engineering feat. The rear wheels turned, just like the front ones. If you look at a picture of this car, you will notice that the rear wheels have a "skirt" or cover over them (as did many cars in the past), and you may wonder how the wheels turn. In actuality, the "skirt" moved outward as the rear wheel turned. The entire top half of the car was all glass, with a removable roof panel. The steering wheel was a twin-grip pod with most push-button controls built right into it. Through a switch on the steering pod, the car could be raised or lowered while driving. It inflated the shocks at lower speeds to avoid bump surfaces and lowered them for improved aero-dynamics and fuel economy on smooth high-speed roads. The driver didn't have to glance down at the instru-ment panel to check speedometer or other warning signals. There was a "head-on" display–or holographic image–on the windshield of all the instruments. When entering and exiting the Pursuit, an "exit" button moved the seat rearward and tilted the interface unit upward simultaneously. While the door was open, it exposed a platform on the seat which assisted the occupants into and out of the car. For entering and exiting the rear seats, the front passengers' seat back pivoted toward the con-sole so the occupant could step over the front seat cushion instead of around it. The rear seat featured an in-tegrated child seat which folded out of the rear seat back. On the back of the front seats' headrests, directly in front of the rear passengers, were two portable mini color television sets with headphones for rear passenger entertainment.

If you ever felt like giving the driver behind you a few well-chosen words for tailgating you, you'd love this vehicle. Among its dozens of exotic devices was an illuminated sign mounted between the taillights which could be programmed by the driver to say anything, like "Dangerous to Pass," "You Are Too Close," and so on. Or perhaps, "Stay Off My Back, You Jerk." It was actually a big electronic bumper sticker. Among Aerostar's dozens of electric gadgets was a "personality" key. This not only unlocked the doors and ignition, but carried a computerized message that told the van which member of the family was climbing behind the wheel. Instantly, the seat, steering wheel, safety belts, floor pedals, and mirrors adjusted to the driver's taste. "Privacy glass," imbedded with liquid crystal, allowed the driver to immediately fog up the side and rear windows at the push of a button. Brake and accelerator pedals could be adjusted up to four inches so that a short-legged driver could position himself comfortably behind the steering wheel. Aerostar had an air suspension system that smoothed road bumps and automatically maintained a constant, level ride height regardless of how the vehicle was loaded. The van had a center console, for holding drinking cups. This was mounted on tracks and could be pushed back within reach of rear passengers.

1987
Oldsmobile Aerotech

This extremely aerodynamic research vehicle was designed not for styling and aesthetics, but for evaluating such engineering aspects as high speed, stability, and the punishment an engine could take under various conditions. Aerodynamics and performance were the primary targets. On August 27, 1987, A. J. Foyt, four-time Indianapolis 500 winner, established a new world closed course speed record of 257.123 mph and a new world speed record for the "flying mile" with an average of 267.399 mph. Both records were posted at the Fort Stockton Test Center at Fort Stockton, Texas. The engine tested in the Aerotech was General Motors' new 2.3-liter Quad 4 double overhead camshaft, 16-valve, 4-cylinder

powerplant, first offered on the 1988 Olds Cutlass Calais and later on other GM cars. Among that engine's new engineering advances are the elimination of spark plug wires and distributor, and other parts. Plugs are sealed with a cover. A computer system monitored thirty-seven channels of information on the engine, chassis, and body. The Aerotech was so low-slung it resembled a racing car It was only 40.1 inches high and had a ground clearance of .5 to 1 inch. The design of the Aerotech included the capability of adjusting underbody sections to control the distribution of downforce front to rear.

167

1 9 8 7
GM Sunraycer

In 1987 General Motors entered an odd-looking solar-powered vehicle in a grueling 1,950-mile race in Adelaide, Australia. It won, and it proved, among other things, that a sun-powered car is a possibility for the future. Resembling a huge teardrop, the one-seat, four-wheeled Sunraycer was driven by 7,200 solar cells. GM entered the race as a practical technical project to develop and demonstrate technology in lightweight structures and materials, low-speed aerodynamics, high-efficiency batteries, lightweight motors, and solar cells. Although nearly 20 feet long, the entire car, with lightweight plastic skin and aluminum tube framing, weighed just 390 pounds. It was propelled by a single direct-current motor weighing 8 pounds and taking up no more space than a coffee can. The motor used a new powerful magnet developed by GM. Called Magnequench, the magnet is so powerful that GM is now using it to crank motors in pickup trucks. But the potential applications of the magnet go far beyond just starting motors. GM says it could be used in such applications as furnaces, refrigerators, washers and dryers, telephones, television, and even hair dryers. The Sunraycer used bicycle tire technology and a technique for braking that actually fed energy back into the batteries. The left rear wheel, which was the drive wheel, ran the drive motor as a generator when the driver took his foot off the accelerator, thus feeding energy back into the batteries.

1987
Chevrolet Express

The Chevrolet Express is what you picture your very own private bullet train might be like. It's a streamlined, whisper-quiet, turbine-powered, ground-hugging, four-passenger, 150-mile-per-hour alternative to the hassle of short-distance air travel. The prospective customer for Express would live in a large metropolitan area, have a long daily commute, and travel often to nearby metropolitan areas. Express offered the convenience of personal mobility, so the commuter would drive it to a special limited-access highway built exclusively for use by Express and similar vehicles (General Motors was, at one time, discussing with the U.S. Government the possibility of building such limited-access roads in the future). Once on this highway, Express would cruise at speeds up to 150 mph. Typical commuting problems such as traffic jams and vehicles slowed by adverse weather conditions would be eliminated. Once close to the destination, Express would leave the limited-access roadway and rejoin the normal traffic flow. The futuristic car incorporated a number of emerging technologies—aerodynamic shape, new materials, new engine, and electronics. Among the novelties were three little television screens (actually cameras) on the dashboard—one in the center and two on each side. They were not for watching the latest TV soap operas, cartoons, or crime shows. The screens reproduced areas around the car for the driver to see—direct rear, left side, right side. Conventional door handles were replaced by a hand-held keyless entry system that raised the roof so the doors could be unlatched.

1 9 8 8
Pontiac Banshee

According to General Motors Corp. designers, this concept car was to suggest what the 1990 high-performance Pontiac Firebird might look like. In addition to a new racy body, the car had a host of innovations in electronics and other equipment not found on other cars—for example, a keyless entry system activated by an infra-red signal from a wristwatch, electric telescoping steering wheel, adjustable spoilers, and a fiery 4.0L V-8 engine. Even the name "Firebird" was to change. Plans were to call it the Banshee (which means a fairy-elf who, by shrieks and wailing, foretells the approaching death of a member of a family). The exterior, constructed of fiberglass skins over a tubular frame, had a sleek, sloped profile and smooth-flowing sides with no interruptions, all glass waas flush-mounted as were the doors, with no door handles or exterior mirrors. The Banshee had a steering wheel smaller than normal for better visibility and contained twenty buttons for radio and other functions (all reachable with your thumb without taking your hand off the rim). The steering wheel telescoped and tilted electrically, and pedals adjusted fore and aft. Other features included a TV monitor for rear traffic; headrest-mounted radio speakers; and a computer showing the road Banshee was on, the terrain, traffic, and data on oncoming cars—and even suggesting the speed to travel.

1 9 8 8
Chrysler Portofino

Originally unveiled at the Frankfurt Auto Show in 1988, the Portofino was created by Chrysler Motors' international design team. Drawing upon the expertise of Coggiola of Turin, Italy, and Lamborghini, the prototype combined advanced aerodynamic styling and body design concepts with the performance of an ultimate European touring sedan. Portofino's engine and powertrain were by Lamborghini. Powered by Lamborghini's 3485 cc V-8, the mid-engine touring sedan had true sports car performance with a top speed in excess of 150 mph. The engine was teamed with an all alloy Lamborghini 5-speed transmission. Portofino's clean, functional styling featured four rotational doors and clamshell opening hood and decklid. The front doors pivoted up and out of the way to allow for ease of entry. Ease of entry for rear passengers was enhanced by the unibody design that eliminated the traditional center pillar. Portofino's interior had an ergonomically advanced driver's cockpit, with a fully adjustable instrument pod, steering wheel, and switch gear. Individual control areas were provided for all four occupants. The car's interior was hand-sewn leather. Ample luggage space was provided in both front and rear compartments. Portofino had independent front and rear suspension, with McPherson struts, coil springs and telescopic shock absorbers, and ventilated disc brakes front and rear.

1 9 8 8
Ford Bronco DM-1

This stubby-looking concept vehicle was originated not by one of Ford's top designers but by a former student at the Pasadena Art Center–Derek Millsap–and was named for him by using his initials, "DM." In a program sponsored by Ford, Millsap and nine other advanced transportation students designed and built clay models depicting their ideas for trucks of the 1990s. Ford executives were so impressed with Millsap's effort that they ordered a full-scale version built by Concept Center California, a design firm that consults with Ford on the trend-setting Southern California market. A multipurpose vehicle designed for driving enthusiasts of the 1990s, Bronco DM-1 is a five-passenger model with a fiberglass steel reinforced body integrating a special roll bar between its inner and outer skins. The vehicle's functional high-volume interior easily seats five adults and incorporates a variety of advanced design concepts, including a special electronic navigational system that maps the vehicle's location via satellite. The Bronco DM-1 has electronic instrumentation done in an analog design to provide the driver the reliability of electronic technology with the easy-to-read features of analog gauges. A secondary "quick-read" digital display at high eye level below the base of the windshield indicates speed, engine rpm, and the time. Primary hand controls for items such as the windshield wipers, rear defroster, and lighting are located within fingertip reach on the outer perimeter of the analog instrument cluster. The rear hatch wraps into the roof line to provide a larger opening for the loading and unloading of cargo.

1 9 8 8
Cadillac Voyage

By no means did this model suggest anything of traditional Cadillac styling. The only distinguishing Cadillac trademark was the hood ornament. A four-passenger sedan, the Voyage had infrared remote-controlled door actuators which eliminated interior and exterior handles and lock cylinders. With it you could make the front windows go down, the rear windows tilt, and the seats and steering column move to an optimum entry-exit position. Other electronic content included a voice recognition (hands off) cellular telephone, high-mounted color CRTs with trunk-mounted camera for rear vision, and a high-mounted color ETAK navigational system with remote switches. There were back and cushion heaters for the driver and even a back massager. The front wheels were half-covered by skirts, or "movable spats."

1988
Lincoln Machete

This car explored sculptural forms not attempted in previous concept car designs. Even the interior was sleek, with all surfaces blending together. Sculpturally integrated deployable lift-control devices were used at both the front and rear of the car. When the devices were deployed, they provided increased down force, which improved handling at high speed. They also provided increased drag, which aided braking. The car featured a "switchable privacy glass," which employed crystals to control light transmission, and darkened for privacy. The headlights and taillights utilized a technology called thin film lighting. Benefits of this design technology were increased trunk and underhood space through component size reduction (50 percent less than today's headlight and taillight assemblies), lower cost, weight, and superior light distribution standards. Rear-vision miniature TV cameras were mounted on both doors and replaced conventional outside mirrors. Through fiber-optic transmission, side and rear-view images would be displayed on two small screens directly in front of the driver. Inside, the driver's seat and center console were all one assembly, furthering the sculptural theme.

1988
Buick Lucerne

This recent offering from General Motors Corp. had a "silent start" engine starting system. Instead of turning a key to start the car, you activated it by touching an infrared control. It utilized linear induction motors. Powered by a transverse-mounted fuel-injected 32-valve V-8 engine, it was targeted for executives forty to sixty years old, with the interior trimmed in burled walnut and leather. In addition to the other usual electronic gadgets, it had a "unified" memory to hold seat, mirror, and power-tilt steering column positions, and a hand-free cellular telephone with computer terminal for the mobile businessperson. Smooth curved surfaces ran from the hood through the windshield and onto the trunk. Some suggested that the overall design had a "Coke-bottle look."

1 9 8 8
Plymouth Slingshot

This old-looking vehicle was designed by Chrysler Corp. for the youth market. In fact, several young people, university design students working as interns with Chrysler Motors designers, made direct and meaningful contributions to the creation of this futuristic vehicle. Slingshot was a lifestyle-oriented vehicle conceived for Plymouth in the image of a high-tech sports car, yet one that was fun to drive. It had a light and rigid carbon fiber chassis, as well as adjustable four-wheel independent suspension. The flexible fenders were positioned right above the wheels for the ultimate in aerodynamic styling. A modular back end, along with exposed frame and engine components, added to the functional appearance. The 2.2 L engine itself featured twin cams, 16 valves, and was turbocharged, yet economical to operate. Slingshot, a charcoal and white vehicle, sat on a 102.97-inch wheelbase. Its overall length was 148.9 inches, and it was 68.04 inches wide and stood 47.69 inches high. Two occupants could ride in an aircarft-style cockpit and were protected by the latest in safety features, including a built-in roll bar, an impact-absorbing honeycomb nose section, high door sills for side impact safety, 125/70 R-15 dual tires on alloy wheels in front, 125/85 VR-16 dual tires in the rear, racing seat belts, and air bags for both driver and passenger. Other features included a keyless credit card system with a pivoting canopy and an elevating driver's seat. Also part of the package were combined headlight and rear-view mirror pods, a six-speed ratchet shifter, and a removable personal stereo.

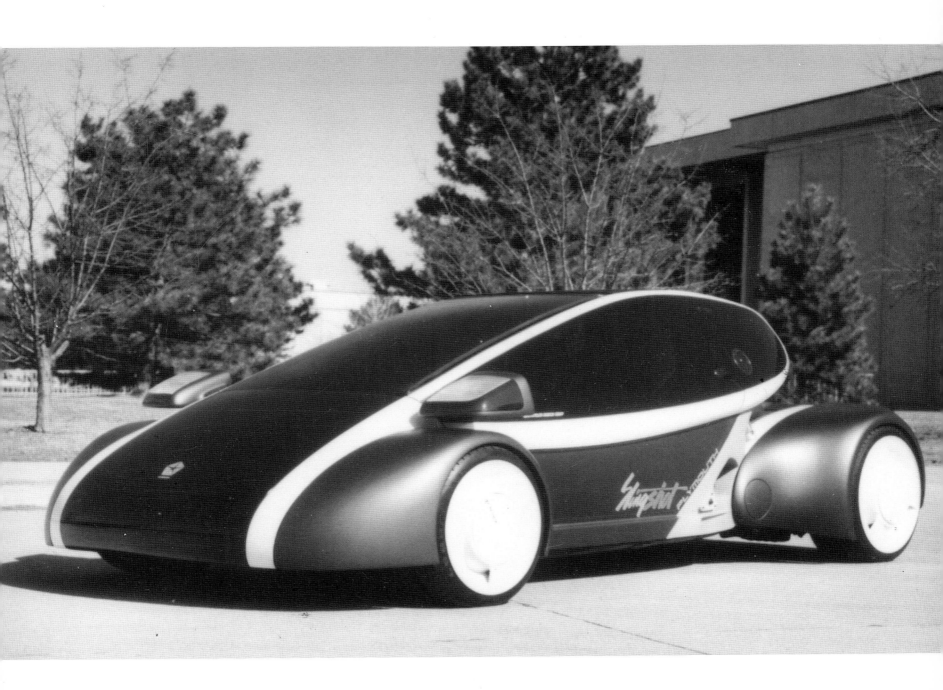

1988
Ford LIV

This two-seat roadster was an experiment in using various new exotic materials in one car, some never tried before. In addition to plastics, components included those made of aluminum, ceramics, and titanium. The letters "LIV" meant "low investment vehicle." The car was built as part of a study to determine if the use of plastic components, and other materials, could reduce investment costs sufficiently to make low-volume popular-priced specialty vehicles economically feasible. The new materials were tried not only in the body, but also the engine and all other components. The conclusion of the study was that plastic components can reduce investment costs. The LIV team also learned there was a five-to-one reduction in the total number of parts and that structural composites can be designed for excellent durability and crashworthiness. Ford notes that only a single LIV car is left today because one vehicle had been cut apart for detailed examination after running extended durability tests and another had been destroyed in a 30 mph barrier crash test, in which it met the government's occupant protection standards. Said Norman A. Gjostein, director of the Ford Materials and Design Analysis Laboratory: "Composite materials utilized in exterior panels and body structural components offer enormous potential. In external panels, we see benefits to the customer in terms of improved corrosion resistance, greater styling flexibility, improved dent resistance, and improved fuel economy through weight reduction."

1988
Chevrolet Venture

An all-glass upper structure was one of the main features of this car. Unusual for a four-door sedan, it had separate lift-off transparent roof panels, both front and rear. Called an "H-Bar," the design offered the security of a sedan with the open, breezy spirit of a convertible. A liquid crystal film darkened the roof panels in direct sunlight. There were no keys for this car. It used an infrared door-opening system. Front seat occupants were treated to a special fifteen-way power lumbar support seat which had a special "massage" setting. For easier entry and exit, the side and lower bolsters folded away automatically. Radio station and telephone numbers were preset and controlled by the driver's voice. As the Venture was being developed, there were also plans to voice-activate other systems, such as heater, air conditioning, lights, wipers and so on. The car had a forward-opening hood for easy access to all routine maintenance components. From an engineering standpoint, the Venture had a modular rear suspension system featuring an integrated transverse composite leaf spring. The type of ride one wanted (soft or hard) could be controlled by a three-position computer unit. Said Chevrolet's General Manager, Robert D. Burger: "Our challenge in developing Venture was to give customers features they'd expect to find in a $30,000 car, but at half the price."

1 9 8 8
GM Centaur

As pickup trucks were rapidly growing in popularity and getting plusher each year, truck firms such as GM Truck & Bus Group, were dolling up their vehicles with glamorous interiors and electronics—each trying to outdo the other in novel innovations. GM's truck marketing theme for 1988 was, "It's not just a truck anymore." And the concept Centaur was probably the best example of that theme—a car-truck. Named for the fabled half-man, half-horse creature of Greek mythology, the all-wheel drive Centaur molded advanced automotive styling and workhorse utility of a pickup into a single all-purpose vehicle. It epitomized America's "truckmania." The Centaur had a smooth, flowing exterior shape and sported a translucent bright metallic red and silver paint scheme. The flush glass and small frontal area provided exceptional aerodynamics. It had a spacious interior with seating for four or five people—two in front and three in back. Unlike those of a conventional car or truck, the instrument gauges were located on a free-standing vertical console which wrapped around the steering wheel to the left. In addition, the center of the steering wheel had pushbutton controls. Car-like engineering features included self-leveling air springs, electric four-wheel steering, and anti-lock brakes.

1 9 8 9
Dodge Viper

When Chrysler Corp. introduced this hyper-muscular 10-cylinder roadster at auto shows in 1989, the company's marketing staff was flooded with written requests for the Viper, some with checks enclosed. Earlier, the import company Mazda had created an automotive sensation when it brought out a sporty little car called the Miata, which was similar in design to the Viper and, thus,

probably created the high interest in such an unusual sportster. The attention the Mazda Miata created just weeks after its debut was phenomenal. However, the Dodge Viper was hidden away. Its future is still in doubt because of strict federal regulations calling for more fuel-efficient vehicles, which the Viper is not. "But stay tuned to us," said Chrysler Motors President, Robert Lutz, a year later at the Detroit North American International Auto Show, from which the Viper was absent. Rakish with open cockpit, it had the plump, powerful, sculptured look of an ancient Corvette. Said K. N. Walling, Chrysler's director of preproduction and international product design: "We said, 'Let's try to go back. Maybe we've gone too high-tech and left some good styling and car concepts behind.' So we looked at those old Jaguars and Cobras. They were very round, but they were also very aerodynamic. This car has V-10 power, rear-wheel drive, a five-speed blood-and-thunder transmission. . . no crazy gadgets. This really is the ultimate Dodge."

1 9 8 9
Plymouth Speedster

Designed to appeal to eighteen- to twenty-five-year-olds, this rear-engine model was intended as a mating of high-performance motorcycles and open sports cars. A molded plastic tube formed a fixed seating surface with seating pads that could be removed so the car could be hosed out for cleaning. Front fenders and hood were combined to form a motorcycle-type faring that wrapped around the front of the vehicle to the door. Within the faring was a pop-up horizontal headlamp bar in the center of the hood and a fixed light bar under-

neath. Speedster's low wraparound windscreen suggested a cross between a motorcycle air deflector and a down-sized roadster windshield. Both steering and foot controls moved fore and aft. All major controls and instruments panels were mounted to the movable steering control fork. Another unusual feature of the Speedster was a running board, which virtually disappeared from automobiles forty years ago but is now making a comeback on some small trucks and vans.

1 9 8 9
Chevrolet XT-2

Here Chrevrolet took an IROC Camaro and put a pickup bed on it. The result: a neat little streamlined utility vehicle. Powered by a 360 hp 4.5L Trans-Am racing V-6 engine, and boasting a Corvette suspension, it pushed along from zero-to-60 in 6.0 seconds, a hot performer for a small truck. Officially, "XT-2" stood for "Experimental Truck #2." The first in the series–the Blazer XT-1–was a four-passenger experimental test bed for future technology on America's favorite sport-utility vehicle. Introduced in 1986, Blazer XT-1 was the first General Motors "show truck."

Given the consumer preference shift to small, sporty trucks, the evolution of the Chevrolet XT-2 Pace Truck was natural. Up front, the aerodynamic windshield was also the hood. The entire engine was located under the windshield, which pivoted up on gas struts for easy engine servicing. Special space-age materials insulated the cockpit from engine heat. In the rear the XT-2 had a removable bed floor for access to the rear drivetrain. The XT-2 stood on 17-inch front and 18-inch rear wheels.

1 9 8 9
Chrysler Millenium

A four-passenger sedan, this experimental car featured scores of safety ideas and, according to Chrysler officials, resembled the Chrysler of the next decade. Said Chrysler: "It's a 'living' research vehicle that explores what safety technology of the 1990s will encompass, as opposed to the add-on approach developed in the 1970s." The Millenium had a mid-engine and a forward placement of the passenger compartment. It featured safety ideas such as traction control, active suspension, infrared heads-up display of information on the windshield, and a navigational system. Among the many other innovations were "anti-submarine seats," or seats which are fixed (driver moves all controls to his preference, such as the steering wheel); voice-activated controls (you tell the car what to do, such as turn on the radio or dial a number on your cellular phone); rain sensitive wipers (they activated when a drop of water hit them); blind-spot radar (which warned the driver if there were any obstacles in the rear or if there was a car approaching from the side which he could not see in the mirror); and a drunk driver disabler (the driver had to punch a certain set of numbers into the computer—if he could remember them—before the car started).

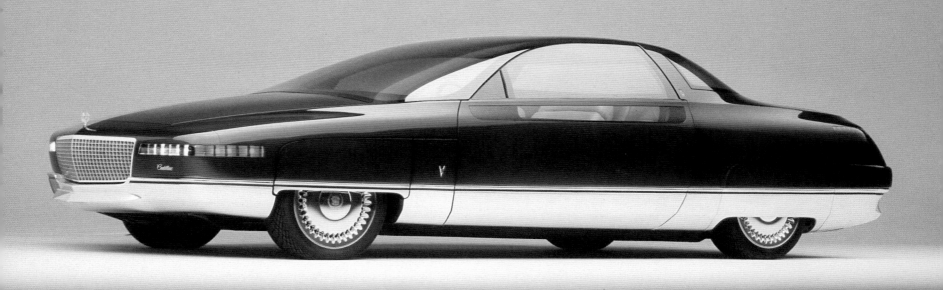

1989
Cadillac Solitaire

This was another General Motors car which company officials indicated could be in production soon. It was powered by a V-12 engine developing 430 horsepower. The upper surface of the car–from the base of the windshield to the rear passenger area– was a continuous piece of high-impact safety-net glass. A unique panel of glass below the beltline presented a very innovative design feature. Body-colored louvers in the front and rear created an illusion of no headlights and taillamps. Solitaire featured possibly the longest doors in GM's history. These doors were uniquely engineered, utilizing a two-piece hinge mechanism which reduced outward door swing and simultaneously moved the doors slightly forward. Easy entrance and egress were possible even in close-quarter situations. When actuating Solitaire's doors, the front windows automatically expressed down as the memory system moved the steering wheel up and moved unoccupied front seats full forward–for ease of rear entry. When the doors were closed, the front seats and electrically powered tilt steering wheel returned to one of three driver-selected memory positions. Its moveable front-wheel skirts served a dual purpose. During normal driving, the wheel skirts were flush with the fenders to preserve the aerodynamic lines. However, when turning maneuvers were required, the wheel skirts extended out to allow wheel movement. Solitaire's absence of outside rear-view mirrors also enhanced the flush exterior design.

1989
Pontiac Stinger

Another one for the youthful spirit, Stinger was an all-wheel-drive and all-terrain performance coupe and convertible. All glass panels on the Stinger could be removed, except the windshield. Even the glass in the lower portion of the door could be taken off and substituted with a panel containing a beverage cooler and storage box. And that's not all. For example, the Stinger had built-in convenience items such as pull-out radio and carrying case, a portable hand-held vacuum, electrical extension cord, camper stove, hose flashlight, picnic table, tool box, carrying case with binoculars, first aid kit, calculator, sewing kit, compass and magnifying glass, fire extinguisher, umbrella, mess kit, two small tote bags, brush and dustpan.

1 9 8 9
Buick Park Avenue Essence

This handsome four-door was probably closer to production than any of the other concept cars. It was said to represent the design direction of future Buicks. The sedan featured a new hinge design that allowed all four doors to be opened extra large, automatic opening and closing of doors, a 5-inch television screen in the rear, a navigational system, and separate climate controls for driver and passengers. A button on the door closed doors automatically. The interior was loaded with other goodies that are closer to production than those of other concept cars. Floor and footwells were large, with power-operated footrests adjustable for comfort both front and rear.

1989
Oldsmobile Aerotech II

In August, 1987, Oldsmobile built a concept car called the Aerotech I, an engineering project that carried race driver A. J. Foyt to record speeds. Aerotech II aimed to apply several of the low-drag benefits of the 260 mph single-seat Aerotech I to a two-door, four-pasenger sports coupe. Aerotech II's silhouette was purposely bullet-like to pierce the wind with the least commotion. This two-door coupe's top surface flowed uninterrupted from the leading edge of a smoothly-molded front bumper, over a 48-inch high roof, to the clean-cut tail section. The extra interior volume provided by the extended roofline was readily accessible through a pair of tinted-glass hatches that lifted upward from each side of the car. Aerotech II was also loaded with scores of electronics gadgets, and front seat passengers were provided with inflatable restraints. One new feature was a ceiling-console-mounted holographic device that projected a red three-dimensional warning on the rear glass panel whenever the brakes were applied.

1989
Oldsmobile Aerotech III

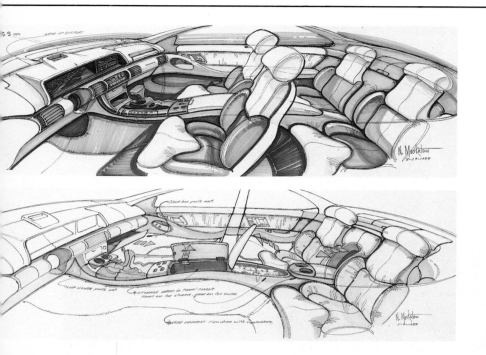

This concept car coddled its occupants in reclining bucket seats for four and had a radar unit that visually and audibly warned the driver in backing maneuvers of nearby fixed objects. It was touted as a touring sedan for the future. Like the original (see page 167), Aerotech III had a low penetrating nose, a comparatively high tail section, and body surfaces designed to slip through the air with minimal disruption. A functional front air dam and deck-mounted airfoil reduced aerodynamic lift and drag forces. Experimental "mini-cube" headlamps offered excellent lighting performance in a very low-profile package. The center-mounted rear brake lamp was integrated into the trailing edge of the roofline. Horizontal ribbing faded away in the midsection of the body to reduce its visual mass. A sliding security shelf behind the rear seats provided the necessary clearance to permit the rear buckets to recline and also ready access to the trunk. A center console ran the length of the interior and provided additional storage space.

1 9 8 9
Ford Saguaro

A multipurpose seven-passenger four-door, Saguaro was designed by Ford's Ghia studio in Turin, Italy. It featured four-sided flush driver and passenger door glass, flush exterior door handles, and a fast windshield angle. The stance of the Saguaro was augmented by 24.8-inch outside diameter tires and 19.4-inch diameter wheels, considered large for such a small car. High-level air intakes were located inboard of each headlight for improved engine cooling during off-road driving. The interior featured two-three-two seating arrangements. Both rows of rear seats folded flat to create an interior cargo area as spacious as an intermediate-size station wagon. The rear liftgate wrapped over into the roof, enabling large objects to be loaded into the cargo area.

1 9 8 9
Ford Splash

This one was obviously for the young who yearned to "splash" around on beaches, scuba dive, ski, surf, or indulge in other youthful activities. Resembling a glorified dune buggy more than a car, this unusual vehicle was designed for Ford by students from the Center for Creative Studies in Detroit. It carried four passengers, had removable windows, roof panel, and hatch. It was only 143 inches long. Other features included retractable high-mount, high-intensity driving lamps for extra illumination needed during nighttime off-road driving. Deployable mud flaps moved up and out of the way during off-road use, but could be lowered into position for highway driving to protect Splash's body from mud and stones.

1 9 9 0
Ford Ghia Via

Ford said this concept car was the first car in the world to incorporate a unique fiber-optic headlight system. Wafer-thin lamp clusters were positioned at the base of the windshield for maximum efficiency. Each consisted of nine separate fiber light units illuminated from a central source, providing illumination equal to a much larger halogen system. The unique headlamps also could be programmed to operate as fog lights or spotlights. The rear spoiler lay flush with the bodywork at low speeds, but was deployed automatically by an on-board computer to provide downforce as speed increased. The design of the rear windows allowed stale air from the interior compartment to be extracted through a small slot. The roof of the Via had a removable Targa-type center section made of photosensitive glass to protect the occupants. The instrument panel used advanced fiber-optic lighting techniques to create a floating effect for the instrument needles. Controls more frequently used were arranged so they could be operated by the driver without removing his hands from the steering wheel.

1 9 9 O
Buick Bolero

As many General Motors designers agree, many of today's mid-size family sedans tend to look bland, so Buick went sporty and streamlined with the concept Bolero, which could go into production in the near future. The rear end is slightly higher than the hood, and the windshield is steeply raked Bolero's sleek appearance is enhanced with slim roof pillars and recessed door frames. Unique to Bolero are the fiber optics used throughout the car, particularly in the taillamps. One fiber-optic light panel extends the width of the rear, with bulbs at both ends. This is a break from the traditional use of taillamp bulbs mounted in parabolas. The Bolero even has a built-in cooler in the rear package shelf, and cup holders front and rear.

1990
Mercury Cyclone

This four-door high-performance concept featured a roof that could be electrically changed from transparent to opaque, allowing the driver to adjust for changes in sunlight. In place of mirrors, two small video cameras transmitted the views from the sides of the car to tiny televisions on the dashboards. Halogen headlamps were in the trunk, their light piped through fiber optics to the front and rear of the car. Solar panels charged the battery.

1 9 9 0
Chrysler Voyager III

Resembling a small Winnebago motor home, Voyager III was two vehicles in one. The owner of one of these could detach the front and use it as a three-passenger mini-car for congested areas. For traveling with more people, he could simply hook up the rear part flush with the front to have room for eleven persons–three up front and eight in back. Voyager III had eight wheels–two up front, four at the rear, and two in the center. The center wheels could retract when the two modules were put together. Actually, Voyager III was not much larger than Chrysler's extended-wheelbase production minivans. Its combined wheelbase was 122 inches and overall length 198.5 inches. The two modules were powered by two electrically linked four-cylinder engines. For minimal power only the front engine would be used. When more power was needed, the rear engine would power it. For maximum power and traction, both engines would be used together. That would be equivalent to a 3.8-liter eight-cylinder engine. At its introduction, Chrysler executives said that they did not expect Voyager III on the market for at least ten years.

1 9 9 0
Pontiac Sunfire

One of the most innovative divisions of General Motors Corp. from a styling standpoint, Pontiac in 1990 sprung out with another eye-popping concept car, the Sunfire. While from a distance the neat car looked like an ordinary two-passenger two-door coupe, it had four doors–the front being standard size while the rear were half size. The rear doors opened toward the rear. There were no center pillars on the doors and no door handles. Instead it featured electronic key fobs and thumb-pad sensitive pressure points. The headlamps were not in their usual location near the grille; they were mounted at the base of the windshield and rotated upward when in use. The upper half of the Sunfire was all glass, which curved from the base of the windshield to the bottom of the rear window. The car featured massive-looking wheels, with thin tires. On the interior the column hub contained controls and displays that rotated with the wheel so they were always upright and readable.

1990
Oldsmobile Expression

Resembling a station wagon more than a passenger car, this four-door sedan did not have a kitchen sink, but it did have a hot and cold storage area and even a built-in vacuum cleaner. On top of that, it boasted an entertainment center in its tailgate area, including a built-in Nintendo game center and mini VCR system. The back seat faced rearward so passengers could view those entertainment frivolities. Seats behind the driver and front passenger folded down flat. Up front there were a console-mounted CRT screen with a Navicar naviga-

tional system. The radio and integral CD player featured separate controls and headrests for each passenger so they could program music of their choice. At the front of the car were five small headlamps on each side. Such tiny headlamps have allowed designers to lower the entire front profile and also provide bright, even lighting of the road surface. The Expression had rain-sensing windshield wipers. It boasted four-wheel steering, and all exterior panels were fiberglass.

1 9 9 0
GM CERV III

Although this concept was mainly an engineering test bed, its exterior styling was an eye-catcher. It was General Motors' third generation car. CERV I had been developed thirty years earlier as a cigar-shaped, single seat, mid-engined sports cars that ran at 206 mph. CERV II appeared in 1964 as a two-seat sports racer designed to explore two new engineering avenues: three-valve combustion-chamber designs and full-time four-wheel drive. The design intent for CERV III was to deliver "remarkable acceleration, braking, cornering, and top-speed capabilities, while easing the driver's tasks." GM called CERV III a "200 mph safety machine." While that characterization at first seems unlikely, it makes perfect sense within the context of a super-performance sports car. CERV III was more than a one-dimensional, dry-road speed machine. It also performed well on wet or slippery surfaces. It automatically corrected for such negative influences on the vehicle as cross-winds, irregular road surfaces, and uneven traction conditions. CERV III purposely did not demand extraordinary driving skills; it was predictable and controllable no matter what driving circumstances were encountered. An average driver could pilot this car quickly and safely without fear that a minor error would result in major consequences.

1 9 9 0
Cadillac Aurora

Many have criticized Cadillac recently for its stodgy and stale styling directed to an older generation of motorists. The average age of a Cadillac buyer is fifty-six. So now Cadillac is trying a radical departure from its current design, with hope of attracting the affluent baby boomers who fancy European cars. The Cadillac Aurora is the first attempt. If results from studies show there is interest in such a car, Cadillac plans to produce the Aurora by 1995. Cadillac calls the Aurora a "high-performance sedan." It carries a 275 cubic inch V-8 engine and a four-speed automatic transmission, but could be a six-speed manual. It's an all-wheel drive. Interior amenities include a navigational system that can store maps for the entire U.S., and a hands-free voice-activated cellular phone. The Aurora has a sunroof the driver can adjust automatically to darken. The Aurora sports no chrome, and the outer body is constructed of fiberglass. Overall length is 190 inches, about the same size as the 1990 Eldorado and Seville.

1990
GM Micro with 2-Stroke Engine

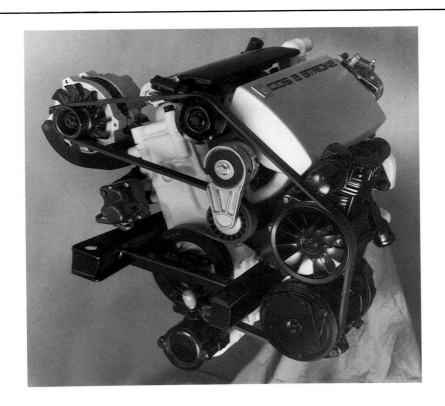

One of the most talked-about new engines by auto companies all over the world has been the two-stroke powerplant. The two-stroker, once little more than a powerplant for lawn mowers and dirt bikes, is the subject of intensive research by U.S., Japanese, and other companies. Since the engine is small, General Motors installed one in a small concept car called the Micro, a shocking bright-yellow model. One key difference between two- and four-stroke engines is that a two-stroke design delivers a power pulse from each cylinder once per revolution. Four-stroke engines require two full turns of the crankshaft to produce one power pulse for each cylinder. Two-stroke engines have several other advantages—more compact exterior dimensions, lighter weight, and fewer moving parts. They also have the potential of producing more power and greater fuel efficiency than a four-stroke engine of equivalent piston displacement. Unlike a four-stroke, a two-stroke engine can be mounted in an upward orientation because its lubricating-oil supply is carried externally.

1 9 6 2
Chevrolet CERV

"Personally, I'm shocked at the 'creative stalemate' I see in worldwide automobile design today. Some manufacturers were introducing totally new cars that are functionally better but look almost identical to the cars they replace. I also see a depressing trend where cars around the world are looking more and more alike. They've lost their distinction, individuality, and personality."

From a 1985 speech made by Charles Jordan,
General Motors Corp. Vice President Design

Index

DATE DUE	BORROWER'S NAME
NOV 1 8 1991	28